VICTORIAN PORTABLE THEATRES

by Josephine Harrop

The Society for Theatre Research
1989

First published 1989
by The Society for Theatre Research
c/o The Theatre Museum
1E Tavistock Street, London WC2E 7PA

ISBN 0 85430 047 3

Printed in Great Britain by
the Alden Press Ltd, Oxford

To Andrew
without whom . . .

ACKNOWLEDGEMENTS

The research for this book has encompassed a wide geographical area and a debt is acknowledged to exceptionally helpful staff at a large number of reference libraries: in particular those at Blackburn, the Bodleian, Bradford, the British Library (both Bloomsbury and Colindale), Halifax, Hull, Preston and Wakefield. Acknowledgement is also due to the Bankfield Museum, Halifax, Halifax Antiquarian Society, the Newcastle-upon-Tyne City Archives Department and the Wakefield County Records Office. I am very grateful to Mary Speaight for redrawing the maps on pp. 35 & 36 and to Mrs J. R. Hodson for permission to use her late husband's reminiscences.

Asa Briggs, Sylvia Harrop, the late Anthony Hippisley-Coxe and Jane Traies were generous with their time and advice and I am in their debt.

Special thanks are due to David Mayer of Manchester University who first introduced me to "Old Wild's" and to Keith Sturgess of Lancaster University who guided and encouraged during the doctoral research which forms the basis of this book.

And finally a special acknowledgement to Dr. Kathleen Barker, the most supportive and helpful of editors.

CONTENTS

INTRODUCTION

The travelling theatres were a nineteenth-century phenomenon. They first came into being around the 1800s, flourished during Victoria's reign and had all but disappeared by the First World War (though a few isolated companies were still to be found up to the 1940s). They were viewed with some disfavour by authority and looked down upon by the established theatre, rarely being regarded in a serious light. Because of this, and also since many proprietors of travelling theatres were virtually illiterate, there is very little primary source material in this field. As a result, the important role that they played in theatrical history has never been fully recognised, and it is to redress that balance that this study has been undertaken.

It should be made clear at the outset that this is not a survey of fit-up troupes nor of circuit companies, which were very different propositions. Fit-up troupes went from place to place carrying their effects with them and playing in public rooms, inns, or barns, "fitting up" their stage within the chosen venue. Circuit companies journeyed from theatre to theatre, usually in a fixed route, opening each for a few weeks before moving on to the next one. This book is concerned with the true travelling theatres or "portables" where the actual structure of the theatre itself, together with stage, scenery, seating and costumes, was carried from town to town, being dismantled, loaded on to waggons, transported and rebuilt at every stop. Independent of established theatres or suitable halls, they were able to travel wherever they wished and alter course to fit changing circumstances. Instead of waiting for their audiences to come to them, they went to their audiences.

The lack of primary material makes this a difficult field to research. One text of outstanding value has, fortunately, survived: *The Story of "Old Wild's"*, reproduced as a companion volume to this book. This account of the life of one travelling theatre has provided a basis from which to work and has made it possible to trace the outlines of a chapter of theatrical history that has been unjustly neglected.* It is inevitable,

*Page numbers in brackets in the text refer to the publication; references to it in notes are indicated by "OW."

therefore, that attention should be concentrated on Old Wild's and on the Lancashire/Yorkshire region where that theatre spent most of its life. Where possible, however, other booths and other regions have been included.

The single most important fact to emerge is that, far from being mere fairground entertainments, the travelling theatres were a genuine alternative home of the drama, competing with established theatres in large towns and bringing the latest plays to villages and remote areas which would otherwise never have experienced real theatre. Until this field is fully researched, the overall picture of nineteenth-century theatre cannot possibly be known. This book is a start; it is to be hoped that others will continue the search and rediscover the old roads travelled by these almost forgotten champions of the theatre.

CHAPTER 1

THE BOOTH

Simple booths for the presentation of plays are recorded from the early eighteenth century, but these were not designed to be taken down and re-erected elsewhere on a regular basis. They were built in one place for one specific occasion or season and afterwards either permanently dismantled or left standing for the next company of actors to use. Booths were erected each year at the large fairs like Bartholomew's or Stourbridge and taken down afterwards; while at Denbigh in 1771, a band of strollers who could not find a suitable place in which to play, asked a local carpenter to build them a temporary wooden theatre [1].

Credit for the first truly portable booth is generally given to John Richardson who as a result of his success in a makeshift theatre at Bartholomew Fair in the early nineteenth century decided to build waggons and take his booth from one fair to the next. It is probable, however, that like so many new inventions similar booths appeared in different places around the same time, conditions being right for their creation. A Mr. Ord, in whose booth Billy Purvis gained early professional experience, was certainly travelling from fair to fair in Northumberland in the first decades of the century [2]. Circuses and other shows were also using portable booths in the early eighteen hundreds (cf G. Speaight, *History of the Circus* 1980).

One of the major factors which influenced the development of the travelling theatre would have been the improvement of the road network through a succession of Turnpike Acts from the late eighteenth century onwards. Prior to these improvements travel conditions were so hazardous that strolling players had enough to do in transporting themselves, their props and their personal belongings from one place to another without taking on the additional burden of heavy waggonloads of timber and canvas.

Another factor would have been the availability, for the first time, of mass-produced industrial materials such as measured planking, ironmongery, tarpaulins, etc., on a wide geographical scale as a result of the

Industrial Revolution. This would have made the actual design and construction of the portable booth a great deal simpler.

The smallest and simplest booths were constructed of poles and canvas, extremely frail and insecure but having at least one advantage over open-air performances in that some control could be exercised over audience payment. Being comparatively inexpensive and also light to carry, they were suitable for smaller companies or one-man shows. David Prince Miller started his career with such a booth and his *Life of a Showman* (1863) records some of the disasters which it suffered: blown into the Tyne, wrecked by drunken miners, carried off on the horns of a bull, and its canvas slit to ribbons by an angry individual who had been denied admission. This last misfortune was one which frequently befell these lighter booths, as demonstrated by a notice on Campbell's booth at Hartlepool in the 1840s:

> Any Person Cutting or Otherwise Destroying Any Portion of this Property will be Prosecuted and a Reward of £1 will be given by Mr. Campbell to any Person giving such Information as may lead to the Conviction of the Offenders. [3]

The majority of booths, however, were constructed on a shutters-and-canvas principle, the wooden shutters being bolted together to form the walls while the canvas was stretched over the top to form the "tilt" or roof. Upright poles, a ridge pole and rafters were used to support the walls and roof, and ropes gave extra stability. The waggons on which the component parts of the booth had been transported were used, once unloaded, to form the supports for the stage and outside parade. A particularly large company with many waggons might use these to form the base of the walls all round, erecting the shutters on top of the waggons. The illustration (Plate 1) shows Parrish's Temple of Thespis at Halifax Fair in 1836 apparently constructed on this principle. A strolling clown interviewed by Henry Mayhew in the late 1840s gives some interesting technical details:

> First we had to measure our distances and fix the parade-waggons. Then we planted our king pole on the one in the centre; then we put our back pole on the one near the parade; then we put our ridge at the top and our side rails; and then we put our tilt up which is for

the roof, and it gets heavy with dirt, and we haul it up to the top and unroll it again, and fasten it again; then we fix the sides up with shutters about six feet square, which you see on the top of the travelling parade carriages. [4]

It was normal for a travelling theatre to attend fifteen to twenty fairs in a season. The dismantling and re-erecting of the booth was therefore a constantly recurring task to be completed as quickly and efficiently as possible. A pleasantly human touch is provided by an account in the *Hull Advertiser* of 11 October 1844 where a reporter, watching the preparations for the fair, head

> a 'persecuted princess' of tonight, yesterday tell her 'tyrannical father' that she would see him — hem! — before she would let him have any more 'yall' till he had put t'roof on!

Mayhew's clown estimated that the "build-up" took from early morning until mid-afternoon and other sources suggest an average of several hours. Sam Wild recalls "pulling down most of the night in order to be able to start off early" (p. 165), and at Boughton Green Fair near Nottingham in the 1840s, one cheapjack complained to another that he would not be able to get any sleep since the theatre folk next door "are now beginning to build up and will be hammering away all night." [5]

Helping to put up the booth was part of the duties of the men in the company, the women being expected to assist with repair work to the tilt and other sewing tasks. The bigger companies often paid an extra allowance for the construction work and Wild's, according to the reminiscences of an anonymous actress who travelled with the show in the 1840s, was particularly well organised in its routine:

> Every piece of [Wild's] large establishment, with its seats, partitions, shutters, poles, props, brackets, flaps, bolts and screws, was numbered; and when packed on the four waggons or trucks belonging to it, was laid in such exact order that it took as little time and labour to build as any small booth then on the road. . . The manager chose six of the actors to help him in building, and paid each man five shillings at every removal. [6]

Some forty years later the Hodson company was paying its workers two shillings a man for the same task [7].

While these wooden booths were undoubtedly sturdier than the simpler poles-and-canvas structures, they were still fairly vulnerable to adverse climatic conditions, the most common mishap being the tearing of the canvas tilt in a high wind. A severe storm at Preston Fair in 1860, which dashed Sam Wild's hopes of a successful season with his newly-formed circus (p. 192), is typical of many such catastrophes. The *Preston Guardian* of 2 June 1860 described the scene with gloomy relish:

> . . . in the Orchard, the havoc was great. Some of the Thespian booths, among which were Johnson's and the unlucky Pickles's, whose former establishment was recently burnt down at Burnley, were unroofed, the scenery and properties inside being a seeming heap of rubbish; and a couple of canvas circuses, Grimshaw's hot-pea establishment, and several stalls succumbed to 'rude Boreas' and their integral portions lay scattered abroad in hopeless confusion. A similar visitation happened on Monday morning and completed the ruin of the previous day. Nearly the whole of the remaining canvas roofs were stripped from their poles and torn to ribbons. . . A group of shivering men with hands in pockets and pipes in mouths were wandering about from wreck to wreck and commenting thereon in language more energetic than refined; many and loud and deep were their wailings at the Fates.

Showmen who had some warning of bad weather usually tried to remove the tilt before it was damaged. Richard Barnard recollected being sent up on to the roof of his family's marionette theatre to loosen the canvas during a strong gale. The wind catching the tilt, he was lifted up bodily and deposited on the ground some distance away [8]. If there were an audience in the booth at the time of the storm, however, removing the tilt was not always feasible. The *Hull Packet* of 14 October 1836 noted that a gale which had swept the fairground the previous night blew in the side of Gould & Hewitt's booth, "the scenery and properties being dispersed among the audience".

Bad weather was a constant enemy to the travelling showmen, but the number of instances recorded of gallery, platform and even stage collapses suggests that booths were not always put up with the strictest regard to safety and security. Sam Wild mentions an incident at Keighley when the entire audience was precipitated into the pit (p. 186); the *Bradford Observer* of 15 December 1842 records the front platform of a booth crowded with fairgoers giving way, when "several limbs were broken". Harvey Teasdale, in his *Life and Adventures* (1867), describes several such calamities: a falling gallery, the collapse of the entire set during a particularly vigorous sensation scene, and, on one particularly memorable occasion at Sheffield, the disappearance of the stage itself:

> The play of 'The Green Bushes' came out, which necessitated the lengthening of the stage floor. Our theatre was in what is called the Castle Yard, and this new portion of the stage came right on to the wall at the back. This wall stood a great height above the houses in the street below, and from some cause or other it gave way and brought part of the stage along with it into the street.

One of the worst gallery incidents recorded occurred not in a theatrical booth but in a somewhat similarly constructed temporary circus building. At Leeds in 1848 the gallery of Pablo Fanque's circus gave way and crushed the people underneath: among the dead was Mrs. Fanque while the wife of Wallett the clown was seriously injured. At the inquest, reported in the *Wakefield Journal* of 24 March 1848, it was stated that the accident had occurred through a major cross-beam being fastened in place merely with nails instead of with iron plates and screws.

Sam Wild describes his family's first booth, in the 1820s, as being "not much bigger than a pea saloon" (one of the little covered stalls which sold boiled peas on the fairground) (p. 13). This would have been one of the simpler canvas structures. By the 1830s, Wild's has progressed to a booth some 80 feet long by 45 feet wide (p. 23). This was fairly spacious, but not the largest on the road at that time: Sam himself observes that Parrish's show was "much larger, if I remember right, than ours" and this is confirmed by two advertisements in the *Wakefield Journal* of 3 July 1840. At the top of the page Parrish announces his booth as "The Largest and most Commodious Now Travelling in Europe" while directly underneath Mrs. Wild declares hers to be "Not the largest in the Kingdom, but for Ease and Convenience to the Auditory, the Best now Travelling".

By the 1850s the Wild booth had grown considerably, being then 104 feet long and 48 feet wide. It was 24 feet high at the ridge, sloping to 15 feet at the side rail. The shutters which formed the sides were 10 feet tall, the extra height being provided by the rails and rafters which raised the roof above the level of the shutters. The parade in front extended the width of the booth and measured 24 feet in depth [9]. Contemporary evidence suggests that it was by this time one of the largest travelling theatres in the north of England: a comment in the *Preston Pilot* of 29 May 1858 is typical:

> Wild's 'pavilion' towered over all the other shows and, like a giant among pigmies, frowned down on its lesser competitors.

The booths of both John Edwards and Samuel Pickles were smaller than Wild's [10] and while no precise measurements are available for these, another (unidentified) portable of the same period is described by the anonymous actress quoted above as "a miserably shabby Booth not above forty feet in length and twenty in breadth".

A comparison betweem Wild's and the most famous of travelling theatres, Richardson's, yields some interesting information. All contemporary references to and illustrations of Richardson's booth emphasise its enormous size. The outside parade is shown as very extensive, continuing around the sides of the building. William Hone, however, recorded that while the outside parade was fully 100 feet in width (considerably wider than that at Wild's), the theatre itself was only some 100 feet long by 30 feet wide. This indicates that for maximum effect Richardson's booth was placed sideways on to the main passageway of the fairground, with the front parade running along the side of the booth. In an 1808 engraving by Rowlandson and Pugin, the patrons are shown coming into the booth near the stage which implies that this was where the parade and steps were sited; whereas in the more conventionally-placed booths the main entrance from the platform led to the back of the gallery [11].

It is not possible to be certain about the capacity of either theatre since audience figures were habitually exaggerated, but evidence does suggest that Wild's was the more spacious of the two. At Bartholomew Fair in 1826 it was observed that

> Mr. R's receptacle for the lovers of the drama is capable of containing 1500 of our suffering fellow creatures, and he is said to have averaged 1200 at each performance. . . [12]

whereas *The Era* of 11 August 1861 noted of Sam Wild's benefit performance at Wakefield: "Between 1600 and 1700 people were present, and the place was crowded to suffocation".

All in all, it is likely that whereas Richardson's concentrated mostly on outside display with its enormous parade, Wild's was actually the larger of the two in terms of both audience capacity and stage dimensions, and may indeed have been one of the largest in the country. Also, Richardson's large booth was brought into use only for the biggest London fairs such as Bartholomew's or Greenwich. For less important venues, a smaller booth was used. (It should perhaps be noted here that by the time Wild's had reached its maximum size, Richardson's was being run by Nelson and Lee, Richardson himself having died in 1836. The booth, however, was the same one that had been used by Richardson.) [13]

The evidence available on the costs of setting up a booth points, as might be expected, to a wide variation according to the size and quality of the structure. David Prince Miller's first booth, for instance, purchased from Billy Purvis, cost £2. A strolling actor interviewed by Henry Mayhew estimated that a good booth could cost anything between £50 and £200 but added that some of the larger ones were even more expensive. The overall value of Wild's in 1851, presumably including scenery, costumes and props, was put at between £300 and £400. [14]

Repairs, particularly to the roof, were a recurring expense. When Samuel Pickles' theatre was wrecked by the storm at Preston in 1860, he said it would cost him "ten pound" to put on a new tilt. Seven years later Sam Wild calculated that it would require at least £30 to provide a covering for the booth "such as I generally had". The threefold increase in cost might be due principally to the difference in size of booth but may also indicate that Wild's normally used a better quality or heavier type of canvas than did Pickles [15].

One of the most important features of the exterior of the booth was the parade or promenade where the company assembled to attract an audience. Here they gave a brief free show, sample of the delights to be found within; when this finished, the patrons ascended to the parade, paid their money, and entered the theatre. Access to the parade was by means of ladders, ramps or flights of steps. Wild's had the added refinement of painted handrails. The entrance door, where the money-taker was stationed, was normally central, although some booths had an entrance at either end of the parade. Another door at the side of the booth served as the main exit, the previous audience being urged out here while the next group entered from the parade. Outside fairtime this side door served as a private entrance to the pit and box seats [16].

At Old Wild's the back of the parade was framed in a painted proscenium with sliding doors. Folding flaps opened out from the sides of the booth, enclosing the parade at each end. These side flaps, together with the back wall of the parade, were painted with colourful scenes depicting stirring military exploits or sensational theatrical denouements. In the competitive world of the fairground it was essential to make as much show as possible, and most booths featured similar pictorial displays. Douglas' theatre had Shakespearean scenes and Parrish described the front of his booth as "a beautiful Picture Gallery, selected from Views in the East and on the Rhine by the Most Eminent Artists" [17].

In addition, many fairground shows displayed painted canvases raised on poles above the roof, as can be seen in James Mudd's painting of Parrish's booth. The *Preston Guardian* of 2 June 1855 spoke of "gigantic pictorial representations which almost hid the pigmy theatres from view", while the popularity of patriotic subjects was observed by the *Blackburn Standard* of 19 April 1843:

> Here you might behold Affghans slaughtered by the score, while in another picture John Chinaman was being sent to the right about in double quick time by the 'British Grenadiers'.

The paintings were not always of a romantic or uplifting nature however; the *Wakefield Journal* of 7 July 1848 noted disapprovingly that the local constable had had to confiscate an indecent picture from outside a booth which had, perhaps unwisely, been sited opposite the court House.

The illustrations on the front of Douglas' booth were reputed to have cost "over £70" and Sam Wild paid £100 for the hundred square yards of canvas depicting the storming of Delhi. Smaller shows which could not afford such displays did their best with flags, bunting, or, in the case of David Prince Miller, a pair of secondhand red window curtains [18]. Albert Smith recalled his own childish delight at seeing the proprietor of one minor booth nailing to the front poles a beautiful piece of red festoon, edged with black, and adorned with round ornaments of thin brass, like the escutcheons of bed-posts! [19]

In 1851, the year of the Great Exhibition, Wild's commissioned a new folding front which represented the Crystal Palace and changed the name of the booth to accord with this display. Other travelling theatres incorporated fanciful design into the structure of the booth itself. Thorne's was built "in the form of the Towers of Warsaw" and Templeton's was described as "castellated" [20]. Holloway's moved the *West Riding Herald* of 7 July 1836 to sarcastic admiration:

> The architectural structure of it was *unique* indeed, and certainly attractive, as the crowd before it testified. The style was of a Mixed order — an Egyptian temple supported upon Grecian columns of every order with capitals of no order known to any except an architect, and surmounted by a Chinese pagoda with Gothic spires. . .

The playgoer who ascended the outside parade, paid the admission charge and entered the theatre, found himself at the back of the gallery from whence the seating sloped down gradually to ground level. At Old Wild's the main seating division was between pit and gallery, the former at 6d evidently superior to the latter at 3d. Not all booths observed this system: at Richardson's the accommodation was "without any distinction of boxes, pit or gallery" and at Wardhaugh's the gallery seats were the more expensive, a trench being dug between these and the stage to hold the standing section of the audience (a real "pit", in fact). This was also the arrangement at Rose's booth where there was "a small unsteady gallery for visitors who chose to pay 4d; for 2d customers there was no accomodation but standing room in the mud" [21].

Gallery seating was constructed on a system of planks, uprights and brackets. Access to the various parts of the theatre could be by ramp or rake at the sides, as in Barnard's booth; by a precarious step-ladder between the seats; or simply by stepping from one plank to another [22]. An account in the *Preston Pilot* of 10 June 1854 affords a rare glimpse into the gallery of a travelling theatre (probably Wild's) during fairtime:

Act I Sc. I of The Drama had just commenced, but we are sorry to
say that owing to being at the very remote end of the gallery we had
a very indistinct notion of the plot. And in addition to our unfortunate position, our attention was distracted by a young lady in short
petticoats, scarlet stockings, and a wreath of flowers, who, standing
on one of the benches in the gallery, seemed to personate a modern
Juno, appointed to "rule the gods". A little boy had excited her
wrath, and she intimated her intent of "evving 'im hout" and
instructed a Mercury who stood as check taker at the door, to expel
the offender. As, however, the culprit sat some dozen rows deep in
a very crowded part of "the house", Mercury declined the task and
informed Juno that unless she "eld 'er jaw, 'er feyther should
know", an intimation which so exasperated that queen of the gods
that she disappeared in disgust and we could once more give our
attention to The Drama.

The pit seating was normally the first few rows of planking at ground
level, and the actual number of these more expensive seats varied according to the occasion. At Preston in 1855, indeed, a visitor to Wild's booth
noticed that the pit was "a double row of seats at the top of the ladder"
— i.e., at the back of the gallery. On conveying his surprise to the
check-taker, he was informed curtly, "We reverses it here, sir" (*Preston
Guardian* 2 June 1855). This is probably an indication of a considerable
preponderance of gallery over pit theatregoers on that occasion, since
more could be crammed in at ground level, around the stage, than at the
back.

Once the fair was over the pit seating took up a larger area and in
addition private boxes (not provided during fairtime) were installed.
Playbills for a Wild season at Drypool in 1845, for example, show only
pit and gallery seats on offer during the three fair days (12 to 14 August).
15 August, however, is advertised as the "First Fashionable Night" and
boxes priced at 1s are on offer from that date until the end of the season.
At Holbeck in 1859, where the feast was celebrated on 15 and 16
September, boxes were advertised from 19 September onwards.

The fact that boxes were excluded or included as the occasion
warranted, argues that they can have been little more than light chairs or
possibly free-standing benches. Their exclusiveness, however, was always
marked by some form of cushioning (p. 23). They may also have been

separated from the rest of the auditorium by some kind of rail or enclosure. The addition of box seating half-way through a season would naturally necessitate a reduction in the other forms of accommodation available, since it is highly unlikely that space was left vacant until required. It would be a simple matter, however, to remove the last few rows of plank seating and reallocate the remainder between pit and gallery.

During fairtime, then, the majority of the seating in the booth was of the cheapest kind, normally designated the gallery. Outside fairtime the proportion of one category to another is more difficult to determine. It has already been noted that Wild's was said to hold between 1600 and 1700 persons when crowded to capacity. Allowing for exaggeration, a figure of 12–1300 might be taken as nearer the mark. The gallery at Wild's held about 800 (p. 186) which would be about two-thirds of the audience. Of the remaining 4–500, the majority would have been in the pit since box seats by their very nature and intent were less crowded than the other kinds.

The more prosperous booths were lined with a warm fabric such as baize which fulfilled the dual purpose of decorating the interior and keeping out draughts. Some also had a brightly-coloured under-tilt to hide poles and rafters and act as an extra protection against inclement weather. In the colder months, coke braziers were used to heat the auditorium. Old Wild's was advertising these as an added attraction at Leeds in the winter of 1835, and Joe Randel Hodson recollected patrons roasting chestnuts in his parents' booth some fifty years later [23].

As mentioned earlier, both stage and outside parade were supported on the waggons which were used to transport the parts of the booth from place to place. This would have raised them some four to six feet from the ground. The stage occupied the full width of the theatre: at Wild's this was some 48 feet and the stage was 30 feet in depth. There were wings and a curtain as in permanent theatres, and the scenery was in the form of hanging cloths suspended on battens. The front of the stage was usually framed in an ornately decorated proscenium: Wild's was described by the *Preston Herald* of 29 May 1858 as being "neatly painted, presenting a better appearance than many Theatres Royal we could name", while Rose's booth boasted a large oil painting, said to be that of Garrick, over the stage. At a booth known as the Sans Pareil, visited by Wilkie Collins in Redruth, "a giant-sized knight in full armour, with powerful calves, weak knees and an immense spear" was painted on either side of the proscenium [24].

Space in the wings can only have been limited while dressing facilities (or the lack of them) varied from booth to booth. Mayhew's clown travelled with a company whose performers dressed underneath the stage, a piece of sacking dividing the sexes. In Rose's booth, according to the anonymous actress quoted above:

> the men dressed on the left-hand side of the stage and the women on the right, a rule that holds good in most booths; the property man adjusting rocks, cottages or any set pieces that he could lay hands on to form a temporary 'tiring room for the latter, the partition being, of course, removed before the play began.

In the eighteen-hundreds all theatres, whether portable or permanent, relied entirely on candles or oil lamps for illumination. By the end of the century electricity was becoming widespread. The period in between was the great age of gas lighting. There was, however, no definite point at which one stopped and the other started, and not even a general date can be assigned to the replacement of candles by gas. In London, for example, both Covent Garden and the Olympic installed gas lighting in 1815, but the Theatre Royal in the Haymarket did not adopt the new technique until 1843 and Sadler's Wells waited until 1853 [25]. Travelling shows, however, were quick to realise the possibilities of the new medium and adapted to its use with surprising speed.

When the young Edward Stirling visited Richardson's booth in the 1820s, oil lamps and candles were still the only source of light. Stirling, incidentally, was of the opinion that the dresses and features of the actors "came out more strikingly" by oil light than they ever did by gas [26]. At Bartholomew Fair in 1825, however, William Hone observed the new invention displayed at Clarke's Circus:

> The spacious platform outside was lit with gas, a distinction from the other shows in the fair, which extended to the interior, where a single hoop, about 2'6" in diameter, with little jets of gas about an inch and a half apart, was suspended over the arena. [27]

This may have been a novelty at Bartholomew Fair but it had already been introduced to fairgoers in the north of England. The *Hull Advertiser* of 15 October 1824 carried an announcement to the effect that at Hull Fair Cooke's Circus would be illuminated by "A SUPERB GAS CHANDELIER". This is one of the earliest records of gas being used to light a travelling show and it is interesting that it predates the London one by nearly a year.

In the early 1830s Wild's booth was still being lit by candles which were used for both stage footlights and a chandelier in the auditorium (the custom of darkening the auditorium during performances was not adopted until late in the century). David Prince Miller, travelling at the same period, described a simple theatre chandelier as consisting of "six pieces of lath nailed across, and nails driven in for sockets", adding that any gentleman who sat underneath would be spared the expense of bear's grease for a long period. Miller's chandelier held a dozen candles; Wild's, which supported forty, was a much larger and brighter source of illumination [28].

By 1835, however, Wild's had embraced the new medium as by November of that year they were using it in the booth at Leeds (p. 28). Other portables fullowed suit: the *Hull Advertiser* of 18 October 1837 noted:

Thorne's melodramatic establishment has started with great splendour; the aid of gas has been called in to heighten the effect of tinsel. . .

The main factors governing the use of this new form of lighting by the travelling shows were firstly the existence of gas manufactories in the towns visited and secondly the willingness of those industries to provide a supply to the fairground or individual booth. (It is surely no coincidence that Campbell's booth at Hartlepool in the 1840s was located "near the Gas House" [29]). Halifax, Leeds and Preston were among those providing the facility to shows from the early 1830s; at Hull, as we have seen, it was available from the 1820s. Smaller towns like Armley, Holbeck and Hunslet, being in effect suburbs of Leeds, also had gas supplies from an early date. Others, however, lagged behind. At Blackburn, for example, the showmen had to make do with candles and oil lamps until 1861. On 30 March of that year, the *Blackburn Patriot* announced:

EASTER FAIR.... Within the last few days, gas-pipes have been laid down in the Market ground from meters in shops adjoining for the purposes of lighting the stalls with gas instead of naptha. This change will be a great improvement.

Exasperatingly, no records appear to have survived of charges by or payments to local gas companies for supplies to the fairground. Wild's, however, was certainly provided with a gas meter plus key in the 1860s at Hunslet [p. 178].

Whether from lack of resources or through disinclination, some booths continued to use candles as the principal mode of illumination until the second half of the century. At Redruth in 1850, the lighting in the Sans Pareil was provided by "tallow candles stuck round two hoops" which necessitated the frequent appearance of a youth to snuff the wicks. In Lancashire around the same time one of the poorer booths relied solely on "two flaring fat pans" to provide all the lighting, the pans being moved from the outer parade to the inner stage at the commencement of the performance. These fat pans, or "fat pots" as they were sometimes called, consisted of three prongs in a tin dish. Rolled-up rags were fitted on to these prongs and lumps of tallow were packed all around. When the rags were lit, the tallow melted and supplied the wicks with fat [30].

In the early days of gas lighting the booth was illuminated in much the same way as it had been in the era of candles, i.e. footlights and a chandelier with, occasionally, a row of lights mounted on a batten. There must also have been some form of lighting at the sides of the stage, similar to the wing lights in major theatres of the period. An inventory of goods taken at Wild's in 1856 included both an "old pipe for inside stage" and a "new gas pipe". The suggestion here is of a single length of pipe in each case which makes it more likely to have been used for footlights. There are several references in Sam Wild's memoirs to footlights whereas the only allusion to what may have been wing lights is in the description of a "great sensation snow scene" in *Janet Pride* which was played "with paper lamps in flaring perspective down the stage" [31].

Although the lighting layout may have been similar, the use of gas would have made stage lighting far stronger and brighter than it could ever have been when candles were used. In addition, gas would have been much more adaptable for special effects. The problems this posed for the staging of plays on a circuit which included both towns which did and towns which did not provide gas are interesting and will be referred to again in Chapter 5. Another major development made possible by the advent of gas was in outside illumination and decoration. Hitherto flares and oil lamps had provided fairly basic external lighting, but now many new, crowd-attracting effects could be created. Old Wild's possessed, in addition to its name in lights, a star and the patriotic letters "V.R." (p. 134) and as early as 1842 the booth was optimistically advertised on Hull playbills as "Brilliantly Decorated with 1000 Gas Lamps".

The Winter Theatres

In the bleak winter months when few fairs were held, some travelling theatres pitched their booths in one town for a lengthy period while others took over an already existing building and performed there until the spring. During the 1820s and '30s Old Wild's used, during various winters, a small theatre in Bradford, a converted chapel in Rotherham and a circus building in Preston. From the 1840s onwards, however, the company adopted the policy of having its own winter quarters built. The Liver Theatre at Bradford was the first building to be thus commissioned and from then on purpose-built winter theatres were the rule rather than the exception, marking the gradual expansion and increasing prosperity of Wild's. Little detail can be found on winter theatres built by other travelling companies but it is likely that most of the larger ones followed the same practice as Wild's [32].

Winter theatres were normally built by local workmen in the chosen town in much the same manner as the semi-permanent circuses erected in strategic locations by showmen like Batty, Hengler or Ryan. Like the booth they were constructed principally of wood but were perhaps sturdier, it not being necessary to allow for frequent dismantling and re-erection (although on at least one occasion Sam Wild moved a winter theatre from one location to another). The roof might be tiled, as at Carlisle in the winter of 1849–50, or asphalted, as at Dewsbury in 1857. Some of these buildings, indeed, were sturdy enough to stand for many years; both the Carlisle and the Dewsbury theatres were sold to other managements and the Liver was not demolished until 1867. The New Theatre at Huddersfield, however, built in the winter of 1862, was pulled down as soon as the company had moved out the following spring in order to realise the value of its timber [33].

The Liver at Bradford had a stage 45 feet wide by 30 feet deep and the building had an overall audience capacity of 12–1300. The Victoria at Dewsbury was 90 feet long by 43 feet wide and could "safely accommodate 2,000 persons", while one at Burnley was 90 by 45. These dimensions match almost exactly those of the portable booth and indeed it was the normal practice for scenery, seating and sometimes even the stage to be transferred direct from the booth to the winter building which was, in many cases "little more than a wooden shell". In view of this, it is not surprising that the evidence suggests the cost of a winter building to be considerably less than that of a booth. Sam Wild claimed that the Carlisle theatre had cost £100 and that at Burnley "at least £200"; and these figures are likely to be exaggerated since he was quoting them in support of an application for a licence [34].

It is unlikely that a great deal of outward display was made on these winter theatres since the company was no longer competing with other shows on a crowded and noisy fairground. An old Bradford resident recalled the Liver Theatre as "but a shabby concern", and even Sam Wild confessed that it had "nothing grand about it". Inside, however, some effort was made to render the theatre attractive and comfortable, especially for the patrons of the best seats. The boxes were lined with baize and their seats cushioned. At Dewsbury this was carried out in a patriotic colour scheme of red, white and blue, and the stage was provided with "a splendid new curtain of crimson and gold" [35]. Ornate and exotic decorations were an attraction in themselves to the audience, many of whom lived in dreary surroundings and the management was well aware of this, as may be inferred from a playbill dated 2 February 1855 extolling the delights of one of Wild's purpose-built theatres at Bury:

> The proscenium, stage doors, etc., are all newly designed and decorated, and of the most magnificent description. The superb embelishments [sic] have been designed and painted by Mr. Fitzgerald, artist to the establishment. The whole has been executed regardless of cost, and the public may rest assured that every exertion has been made to present a combination of chaste decorations that may defy competition.

The reference to stage doors is interesting, suggesting that these were still in vogue in the 1850s; there is no record, however, of their inclusion on the booth stage.

As already mentioned, seating was normally transferred from booth to winter theatre and would thus, in most details, have been identical to that provided for summer audiences. Boxes, however, were a permanent feature of the winter buildings and would therefore have been built in a more traditional form, separated from the rest of the house. At Bury they were graded into Front and Side Boxes at 1s6d and 1s respectively, and at Dewsbury into Upper and Side which suggests a tiering system. William Scruton described the "dress boxes" at the Liver as "small and stuffy":

> looking very private and select, no doubt, but very much like so many shut-up beds.

At Burnley an extremely large side box was installed, rather more of a general seating area than a small exclusive enclosure, since it was capable of holding forty or fifty people at a time [36].

Overall the proportion of gallery seating remained about the same as in the booth, that is approximately two-thirds of the whole. Box accommodation, however, was increased with a corresponding decrease in pit seating. The implications here for a change in the type of audience will be discussed in Chapter 3.

As winter theatres were purpose-built and often remained standing for many years, it would have been comparatively simple to arrange for a gas supply — provided, of course, that the town in question possessed the facility. All the towns chosen by Wild's for winter seasons were in heavily-industrialised areas and had their own gas companies from an early date. It can be assumed, therefore, that gas was the normal lighting medium in the winter theatres built especially for the company, although where already existing structures were converted for winter use this may not have been the case.

The winter theatre, then, was very similar in both size and facilities to the portable booth, often being designed to incorporate the booth's interior fittings. It was not just the onset of winter that spurred the travelling companies to move into these buildings, however; after all, there can have been little actual difference between a good booth and its static counterpart. Several factors contributed, among them contemporary legal strictures and the prevailing attitude to "strollers". These will be discussed in later chapters.

REFERENCES

1. Price, C., *The English Theatre in Wales in the 18th & Early 19th Centuries*, 1948, 35.
2. Rosenfield, S., "Muster" Richardson — 'The Great Showman', *in* D. Mayer & K. Richards (eds.) *Western Popular Theatre*, 1977, 108. Arthur, T., *The Life of Billy Purvis*, 1875, 19.
3. Notice, undated but c. 1840s, Wood Collection, Newcastle-upon-Tyne.
4. Mayhew, H., *London Labour and the London Poor*, first pub. 1851, this ed. 1967, Vol. III, 128.
5. Green, W., *The Life and Adventures of a Cheapjack*, ed. Charles Hindley, 1876, 98.
6. Anon, article in *Chambers' Journal*, 4th Ser., no. 74, 27.5.1855. Quoted in Traies, J., *Fair Booths and Fit-ups*, 1980.
7. Hodson, J. R., *Memories of 90 Years in the Theatre*, c. 1975, MS. in the possession of Mrs. J. R. Hodson.
8. Speaight, G. (ed.), *The Life and Times of Richard Barnard*, 1981, 15.
9. *Chambers' Journal, op. cit.*
10. O. W., 96 and *Preston Herald*, 29.5.1858.
11. Hone, W., *Hone's Everyday Book*, 1825, Vol. I, Col. 1182.
12. Quoted in Mahard, M. R., *The Fortunes of a Penny Showman*, Harvard, 1982, 214.
13. Rosenfeld, S., *op. cit.*, 110.
14. Miller, D. P., *op. cit.*, 91. Mayhew, H., *op. cit.*, 140. O. W., 103.
15. *Preston Guardian*, 2.6.1860. O. W., 233.
16. *Chambers' Journal, op. cit.* & playbills, Hull Central Library.
17. O. W., 131; *Chambers' Journal, op. cit.*, Mayhew, H., *op. cit.*, 130, *Wakefield Journal*, 3.7.1840.
18. Mayhew, H., *op. cit.*, 140; O. W., 164; Miller, D. P., *op. cit.*, 58.
19. Smith, A., *A Little Talk About Science and the Show Folks*, 1855, 112.
20. O. W., 25 & 98; *Leeds Intelligencer*, 15.7.1854.
21. Hone, W., *op. cit.*, col. 1182; Slater, T., *Reminiscences of an Actor's Life*, 1892, 33; *Chambers' Journal, op. cit.*
22. Speaight, G., *op. cit.*, 21.
23. O. W., 23, 28; Speaight, G., *op. cit.*, 19; Hodson, J. R., *op. cit.*
24. Collins, W., *Rambles Beyond Railways*, first pub. 1851, this ed. 1982, 120.
25. Rees, T., *Theatre Lighting in the Age of Gas*, 1978, 9, 16–17.
26. Stirling, E., *Old Drury Lane*, 1881, 25.
27. Hone, W., *op. cit.*, col. 1175.
28. Miller, D. P., *op. cit.*, 25; O. W. 23.
29. Playbill, undated, c. 1840s, *Wood Collection*, Newcastle-upon-Tyne.
30. Collins, W., *op. cit.*, 120; *Chambers' Journal, op. cit.*; Sanger, G., *Seventy Years a Showman*, 1910, 75.
31. O. W., 134–5, 23, 178, 223.
32. Scruton, W., *Pen and Pencil Pictures of Old Bradford*, 1890, 127; O. W., 21, 39, 55.
33. O.W., 187, 87, 143; *Era*, 31.3.1850 and 28.11.1858; Scruton, W., *op. cit.*, 135 and Mellor, G. J., *Theatres of Bradford*, 1978; O. W. 208.
34. O. W., 55, 128, 166; *Era*, 28.11.1858 and 27.11.1859; *Carlisle Patriot*, 1.12.1849.
35. Scruton, W., *op. cit.*, 135; O. W., 55, 141.
36. O. W., 141, 166; Scruton, W., *op. cit.*, 136.

CHAPTER 2

THE CIRCUIT

The essence of the travelling theatres is that they went to their audiences instead of staying in one place and waiting for their audiences to come to them. The history of any portable is also the history of its journeyings and the places it visited.

The main considerations to be borne in mind by the travelling showman when planning his route for the year ahead were laws, roads and fairs; that is, the current legislation affecting theatrical performance, travelling conditions, and the annual calendar of feasts, fairs, and other local celebrations. A good working knowledge of all three was essential in order to map out an effective circuit.

Nineteenth-century theatrical legislation is a complex topic but insofar as it affected travelling theatres the main points will suffice. At the time that Jemmy Wild started out on his showman's career, the Act of 1787 was in force. This allowed justices of the peace to license occasional theatrical performances under certain stringent regulations which included a limit on the duration of the licence, a ban on any such licence being granted within eight miles of a patent theatre, and a ban on more than one licence being issued for the same area at the same time. The Theatres Act of 1843 officially relaxed these regulations, allowing theatrical companies to obtain licences from local justices, provided 21 days' notice was given. In practice, however, there was still a good deal of magisterial opposition and even if application was made, there was no guarantee that a licence would be forthcoming [1]. Fairs, however, had their own courts of law which, for the duration of the fair, superseded the normal legislation. Players performing on a fairground within the official fair days could do so without hindrance. The 1843 Act acknowledged this right officially but the evidence indicates that it had been accepted practice for at least a century before and probably from the time that fair charters were first granted.

Outside fairtime all theatrical companies officially needed to obtain a licence by applying to the local justices three weeks in advance. In practice, portable theatres seem to have had an unofficial system whereby for short periods (i.e. at either side of accepted fair-days or "filling-in" en route from one fair to another), the verbal permission of the Mayor or other local dignitary sufficed. For longer seasons, however, a licence was essential, and in either case the proprietor of the travelling theatre was dependent upon both the goodwill of the local authorities and his own reputation to obtain the necessary permission.

Up to the last years of the eighteenth century most regular travellers journeyed either on foot or on horseback, the condition of even major roads being such that the passage of wheeled transport was always difficult and at times impossible. Strolling entertainers, therefore, tended to travel light, limiting their props and effects to what could be carried by hand. Their journeys too, and the distance that could be covered each day, depended very much on local road and weather conditions.

By the early years of the nineteenth century, however, the work of such men as Metcalfe and McAdam had made considerable improvements. In the region travelled by Old Wild's, for example, the roads between Wakefield and Doncaster, Huddersfield and Halifax, Ashton and Stockport, Bury and Blackburn, had all been brought up to a high standard through the skill of "Blind Jack" Metcalfe of Knaresborough. This meant that waggons and caravans, and thus portable theatres, were now practical propositions for travelling entertainers. Moreover, for the first time it became possible to calculate with some degree of accuracy how long it would take to journey from one place to another and thus to plan a circuit some time in advance instead of from day to day [2].

By modern standards, of course, the roads were still far from good, and delays and mishaps were frequent. Billy Purvis, the Northern clown, recalled how, in the 1820s, on a particularly awkward stretch of road between Rothbury and Bellingham, the waggon stuck fast in the mud, throwing those on top to the ground and necessitating the assistance of a local farmer to haul it out again [3]. Fifty years later, Sanger's circus found conditions little improved :

> The average speed of travel? Four miles per hour, with the elephants sent on ahead because they couldn't go as fast as that. The road surfaces? Occasional level patches of mud or dust islanded among wheel ruts and ridges. [4]

In winter, road conditions were worse and the hours of daylight fewer. Virtually all showmen stopped travelling for the winter, some living in their waggons on what they had been able to save during the summer, some seeking employment in Christmas pantomimes at major theatres, and others, like Wild's, moving into permanent buildings and performing there until the spring.

Although Old Wild's reached its peak of prosperity during the years of the great railway boom, the arrival of this revolutionary method of transport affected its habits but little. Occasionally animals or equipment were sent by train, and Sam Wild used it for personal journeys, but the show continued to move by road. Very few travelling shows, in fact, utilised the railways until the 1880s. Arthur Fenwick attributes this to the type of caravan or waggon in use in the earlier part of the century, which could not be easily adapted to carriage by rail. In the last decades of the century a new type of waggon was developed which was more suited to being moved in this matter [5]. Another major factor, however, must have been the extremely high cost of rail travel. In its early years only the well-to-do could afford it which suggests that Sam Wild must have been comfortably off to make use of it even to the extent that he did. It was not until the 1870s that the railway companies began to see possible advantages in offering cheaper travel.

While the proprietor of a large show travelled with his own living van and a number of waggons to carry the components of his business, the members of his company had to find their own lodgings at each stop and not infrequently had to make the journey on foot, as travel expenses were not met by the management. In the 1830s, when his parents still managed the company, Sam Wild took it as a matter of course that he and other members of the troupe should make their own way from Knottingley to Hull — a distance of some 45 miles — partly on foot and partly by boat, putting up at their "usual lodging house" on the way [6].

When space allowed, the waggons which carried the company's effects could also be utilised as passenger transport, as one of Mayhew's strollers confirmed:

> The women always ride on top of the parade carriages, and the men ocasionally riding and shoving up behind the carriages up hill. [7]

For companies which possessed much luggage but few waggons, the carrier's cart was the solution. Wild's was making use of such a service to send its props and effects from Preston to Blackburn in 1837, which suggests that the establishment was not yet particularly large or prosperous. At a later stage, when the company had sufficient waggons but not enough horses, the latter were hired at one town and left at the next. Hiring rather than owning meant some saving in stabling and fodder bills, but was not by any means an inexpensive undertaking: it cost Sam Wild £50 to move the show from Preston to Halifax, a distance of some 40 miles, in 1850; while in 1864 he was unable to move on from Dewsbury to a new location because the cost of doing so "was a terrifying item which I was not prepared to meet". At the height of its prosperity, Wild's needed 15 horses to get it on the road, whereas Parrish's required "at least 40 horses" to move even ten miles as early as the 1840s. It is significant that not long afterwards Parrish's ran into financial difficulties and had to be sold [8].

To put this into context, it must be observed that the portable theatres had fewer problems than other travelling shows such as circuses and menageries. Wombwell's menagerie, in particular, was frequently in difficulties, the elephant waggon (which alone required fifteen horses to draw it) being the usual culprit. On one occasion the axle-tree gave way; on another the waggon became wedged under a railway bridge and, being extricated from that trap, sank into the soft ground at the side of the embankment, whence it was only hauled out after several hours [9]. When it again got into trouble on the winding by-ways of rural Lancashire, the *Preston Pilot* (3 May 1834) felt called upon to utter a mild reproof:

WOMBWELL'S MENAGERIE. The unwieldy caravans which contain the various animals in the menagerie are not the most suitable for travelling on the narrow paved roads of the Fylde. On their journey from this town to Kirkham at the beginning of this week, owing to an accident, one of the horses had its leg broken. . .
On Wednesday, when the collection was travelling from Kirkham to Garstang, one of the caravans (we believe it was that containing the elephant) was upset near Elswick and it was no little trouble to get it righted; and another of them, when ascending the canal bridge at Garstang, owing to the iron-work which connects the shaft with the undercarriage giving way, fell over, and was within three or four yards of breaking in the roof of a cottage. . .

Plate 1. Parrish's Booth at Halifax Fair, 1836, painted by James Mudé. *Reproduced by courtesy of Calderdale Museum Service, Halifax.*

MR HOLLOWAY as RICHARD III   N.º 99

MR HOLLOWAY AS RICHARD THE 3RD

London Published by J. REDINGTON, 73 Hoxton Street, Formerly called 208 Hoxton Old Town.

Plates 2 & 3. "Penny Plain" and "Tuppence Coloured" prints of one of the Holloway brothers as Richard III. Both James and John played the part for the Wilds. Plate 2 is reproduced by permission of Pollock's; Plate 3 by permission of the University of Bristol Theatre Collection.

Plate 4. Bill showing Sam Wild in a favourite role as Mat Meriton, "every inch a sailor," in Halifax on 28 June 1837. *Reproduced by courtesy of Calderdale Museum Service, Halifax.*

It is interesting that Wombwell's felt it necessary to carry the elephants in closed waggons, even at so much additional trouble and expense. This was in the 1830s; some twenty years later, Sam Wild's camels travelled on foot as part of the general entourage (p. 132) and, as already mentioned, Sanger's elephants and camels were sent ahead of the main body of the show, also on foot. Wombwell's practice may have had something to do with the novelty value of elephants in the 1830s: a value which they feared would be impaired if the animals were too easily viewed without charge.

At the other end of the scale were the very small shows, the proprietors of which could not afford more than a donkey-cart to transport their belongings from one town to another. Some could not even rise to a donkey, as David Prince Miller recalled:

> Imagine yourself to be in my situation: about a hundred-weight of luggage, consisting of clothing for us all, but of a very humble description, a drum, magical apparatus, a box of mechanical figures, an old scene, and other etceteras that we used in earning our livelihood; a fair on the following day, twenty miles distant, funds very low, not more than sufficient to defray the night's expenses, and no means of getting there. [10]

On that occasion, there being no other solution, Miller and his family managed to drag their entire establishment on a hand-cart to the next fair twenty miles away. Not to have done so would have meant losing any chance of saving the situation.

The fairs which in the nineteenth century formed the basis of the travelling showmen's circuits can be divided into three categories (although in practice they amounted to much the same kind of event). These were: charter fairs, hiring fairs and feasts.

Charter fairs were originally established by royal charter for the purposes of trade and conferred upon the holder of the charter the right to levy tolls and dues on all those attending to sell their goods. Strolling players and other entertainers were naturally attracted to these large concourses of people and gradually, as the trading aspect declined, owing to improved transport for goods and the establishment of shops and warehouses, the pleasure fair expanded. At the beginning of the nineteenth century the emphasis was still on trade, particularly in livestock.

By the 1830s, however, the number of entertainers attending these occasions was growing, and by the 1850s the pleasure fair had almost completely superseded the business of trade.

The particular distinction of a charter fair was its right to hold a court of summary justice, the ordinary courts of law in the town being suspended for the duration of the fair. This was known as a "Pie Powder Court", possibly from "pieds poudrés" or dusty feet of travellers. Cases arising out of incidents occurring during the fair were tried and sentence passed immediately. Such a legal arrangement obviously made sense when so many people attending the fair were travellers. It is interesting, however, to note that sentences passed in the Pie Powder Court were usually more lenient than those which would have been imposed under normal law. In nineteenth-century England, when punishment was severe for even the most trifling offences, it made quite a difference to be apprehended inside or outside fairtime. At Hull in 1839, when the fair ceased at midnight on Saturday and recommenced on Monday, those who were arrested for being drunk and disorderly on either of these days were discharged, while the unlucky individuals who were taken on the Sunday were fined [11]. The upholders of normal law and order found the less rigorous approach of fairtime law somewhat irritating, as may be seen from a disapproving report in the *Halifax Guardian* of 30 June 1849:

SINGULAR MAGISTERIAL LAW FOR FAIRTIME: Two travelling thieves, named George Caygill and Elijah Shaw, were committed to the House of Correction for two months as rogues and vagabonds, on the charge of being in the fair with intent to commit a felony. . . On any other week in the year, such a series of robberies would have entitled the thieves to a regular trial by jury, and would, in all probability, have entitled the country to a riddance of the thieves by transportation; but as it was Fairtime, they were committed summarily. On being sentenced to two months, one of the prisoners remarked (as he was going back to the cell) that it was twelve months less than he expected — a remark which exhibits a stronger sense of justice in the mind of a prisoner than existed in the minds of those who first originated this injurious but universal magisterial leniency during Fairtime.

Hiring or Statute fairs — called "Stattys" in the north and "Mops" in the Midlands — were first established under a statute of 1563 which laid down regulations for the hiring of apprentices. They were usually held late in the year (often in conjunction with a winter cattle fair), when servants and farm workers hired themselves out for the following twelve months. Joint cattle and hiring fairs were held at Leeds and at Wakefield in November and at Bradford in December each year. On these occasions, as at charter fairs, the entertainment had grown up around the original purpose of the event; and as fewer and fewer young people offered themselves for domestic or farm service, preferring the better pay and conditions of the factories, the shows became the principal attraction.

Feasts, also known as wakes, tides or rushbearings, had their foundation in the celebration of the feast day of the local saint or the commemoration of the consecration of the local church. At rushbearings a decorated cart bearing sheaves of rushes was drawn around the town: a relic of the time when the floor of the church was strewn with rushes which were renewed once a year. Feasts did not have the official sanction possessed by charter or statute fairs, but in most cases long usage had conferred a certain degree of privilege.

The tolls and dues levied on traders in earlier days had been replaced in the nineteenth century by the rents paid by showmen and stallholders to the beneficiaries of the charter — by that time usually the town authorities. At those fairs for which no official charter existed the rent was paid to the owner of the land on which the fair was held. At Hunslet, for example, dues were collected by the Chief Constable on behalf of the lord of the manor. Similarly at Knott Mill in Manchester, another fair with no official charter, rents were paid to the lord of the manor until the city's incorporation in 1838. Little information is available on the actual charges made for fairground sites: in 1806 James Kite (whose widow married Jemmy Wild), paid a guinea for a week at Knott Mill, and in 1811, his circus having increased in size, he paid two pounds eight shillings. Two years later John Adams paid three pounds three shillings for his pitch [12]. Unfortunately no measurements are available by which a scale of charges can be calculated on the basis of this evidence.

Sam Wild made a practice of booking fairground sites in advance, but not all fairs offered this facility. In some areas preference was given to local showmen, as at Sunderland in 1834 where Billy Purvis was allowed to choose the best site, much to the chagrin of William Thorne [13]. In others it was first come, first served, and if, as was often the case, one major fair followed close upon another, there would be frantic races on the roads between the two locations. Nottingham and Hull are a typical example, the first ending on 10th October and the second starting on the 11th. It was between Reading and Henley fairs, however, that Lord George Sanger witnessed a particularly violent incident:

> About two miles from Reading, on the Oxford road, the trouble began. Hilton's drivers tried to pass Wombwell's. . . All at once one of Hilton's men knocked one of Wombwell's drivers off his seat with a tent-pole. In a minute all was confusion. . . Then the rest of the showmen took sides, for in the profession Hilton's and Wombwell's each had their supporters, and in less than a quarter of an hour, a battle was being waged on the Oxford road, at three in the morning, such as had not been seen since the time of the Civil Wars. Even the freaks took part. The fat man made for the living skeleton with a door-hook; the living skeleton battered at the fat man with a peg-mallet. Windows and doors of caravans were smashed, and men were lying about bleeding and senseless from wounds. [14]

Once on the fairground the travelling theatre had to compete with other shows for the patronage of the holidaymakers. The number and variety of shows depended on the size of the fair: at Halifax or Leeds, for example, there would be two or three of the major circuses like Batty's or Ryan's, at least one of the big menageries and as many as four of the larger travelling theatres. Sam Wild recalled one occasion at Leeds when Parrish's, Thorne's and Holloway's were all drawn up in opposition to Old Wild's. Even at a small fair there would be a considerable number of different shows. Circuses and menageries were the most expensive to patronise, a seat at the circus costing as much as 2s6d (although standing room at 6d was usually available) and admission to a menagerie such as Wombwell's being 2s for adults with children at half price. The bigger portable theatres came next with seats normally at 1s, 6d and 3d, while waxwork and puppet shows were also comparatively expensive, charging between 1s and 6d [15].

There were also many smaller booths and entertainments where admission might be had for a penny. Most of the skills which could be seen together under one roof at the circus could also been seen separately in these cheaper shows: acrobats, slack- and tight-rope performers, trained animals, clowns, etc. Freaks, both human and animal, were popular: among the former, giants and dwarves were common, but albinos, a limbless woman, a two-headed baby, a girl "with the formation of elephants' legs and an elephant's trunk growing out of her right shoulder" and the Pig-Faced Lady are also recorded. The last-named was in fact no lady but a bear with shaved face and paws, appropriately garbed [16]. Animal freaks tended to owe more to the embalmer's art than to nature: one collection displayed at Preston in 1855 contained a six-legged horse (all the hooves carefully shod), a two-bodied cat and a four-legged hen. The *Preston Guardian* of 2 June 1855 warned: "These phenomenons were represented as 'all alive', but those who went inside to view them know different". A variation on the animal show was known as "Happy Families": several animals and birds of widely-differing temperaments were shown living together in the same cage, apparently in perfect amity.

Boxing booths and shooting galleries provided an opportunity for those who wanted to take an active part in the fun of the fair. In the boxing booth the resident champion challenged all comers: if no-one accepted the offer there was usually a staged fight to be enjoyed, like that at Preston in 1852 between Mickey Ben and the Mansfield Slasher [17]. Both Billy Purvis and David Prince Miller were involved with boxing booths in their early careers. In the shooting galleries local sportsmen could test both their skill and their patriotism by taking shots at the enemies of the British Empire set up in effigy.

Then there were the "rides". Roundabouts were still hand-propelled for the first half of the century, steam-driven ones making an appearance in 1867. Swingboats (or "flyboats") were built to take a large number of people at one time: the "Highflyer", for example, which toured the Lancashire fairs in the 1850s, could hold more than 60 [18].

Finally there were the stalls, the last survival of the days when the main purpose of the fair had been trade. Now they sold food and drink as well as "fairings" — cheap souvenirs to be taken home as mementoes. The *Preston Pilot* of 30 May 1863 gives a vivid picture of the delights to be sampled:

> . . .whole streets of gingerbread and nut stalls, toy booths in which were exposed in tempting array tinselled dolls and packthread fiddles, clocks warranted to go for a short time and then stop for good — refreshment booths where original preparations against

famine were vended — pies and pastry, the contents of which looked like peppered India rubber, pigs cheeks and ham, which bade fair to melt beneath the scorching rays of the sun, dirty-looking ice-creams, and black puddings, the compound parts of which could not be analyzed satisfactorily to the stomach. Pop and other gaseous drinks, sufficient to have inflated the whole population and blown them up to any height the atmospheric density permitted.

Each show, booth, ride or stall endeavoured to draw the attention and patronage of the fairgoers to itself. The larger establishments had platforms on which the performers sang, danced, blew trumpets and banged drums. The proprietors of smaller shows had to be content with shouting at the tops of their voices. A strong voice was a great asset on the fairground and one of Richardson's actors, John Cartlich, was remembered for having a voice that had "stilled the din of Old Bartlemy at its wildest" [19].

Up to 1862, when a licence became necessary, alcohol could be sold freely on a fairground. This meant, inevitably, that as the day went on the fair became wilder and noisier, with frequent fights or other disturbances after dark. The *Halifax Courier* of 2 July 1853 commented:

> With regard to "Halifax Fair", there may be something of good in it, but there is also much of harm. . . while it be daylight, it is to a certain extent unobjectionable. But the "night sight" is far from being so acceptable; and it needs but a stroll through the fair field at night to make one regret that the amusements of the people have not in them something more worthy of the time and money bestowed upon them.

Drunkenness was one of the principal evils cited by those who opposed fairs. Throughout the nineteenth century there was a steady stream of books and pamphlets decrying these festivals as occasions for moral profligacy, harking back to a pagan past. The opposition achieved its greatest success in the south of England, particularly in the London area where Camberwell, Stepney, Greenwich and Bartholomew fairs were all abolished in the 1850s. In the north, however, it made little headway — with the one great exception of Manchester and Salford where all four annual fairs were abolished at one stroke in 1876. In many northern towns pressure groups tried to wean fairgoers away from their time-honoured amusements by providing alternative entertainment. At Halifax, tea-drinkings and "temperance galas" were organised, but it is worth noting that on one occasion at least in the 1850s, the event was so poorly attended that the organisers had to invite Pablo Fanque to bring his circus up from the fairground to attract the people. Sam Wild refers to appearing with his dog 'Nelson' at a temperance gala in Leeds which was timed to coincide with the July fair [20].

In the earlier part of the century the fairs were held, as they always had been, in the town centre, around the original market place. As both towns and fairs expanded, however, the disruption caused became greater and the authorities began to make efforts to move the festivities to locations where they would be less of a nuisance. Such efforts are understandable in the light of Sam Wild's casual reference to an occasion at Hunslet when he blocked up an entire street with his booth "and the buses from Leeds had to run 150 yards round in consequence" (p. 209). In some cases the move to a new location was made without difficulty: at Blackburn, for example, where the *Blackburn Standard* of 15 April 1846 noted approvingly:

> The opening of the New Market Place has given quite a different character to our Easter Fair and added materially to its manifold attractions. Blakeley Moor, which was generally so overcrowded with shows, stalls, swings and people that it was difficult to get across, now affords ample accommodation for the many hundreds attracted thither; while the whole of the New Market Place shows a more bustling and cheerful appearance. . .

In contrast, however, attempts to move Wakefield Fair off the public streets were strongly resisted, as shown by this report in the *Wakefield Journal* of 14 November 1851:

> WAKEFIELD WINTER FAIR. During the latter part of last week and in the early part of the present week, the walls of the town have been thickly posted with various notices bearing upon them the ominous letters 'V. R.' and the royal arms. Any stranger would have imagined from the variety of these notices and the authorities they quoted in support of themselves, that it would be a very difficult

matter to tread on unhallowed ground in the town of 'Merrie Wakefield'. One class of announcement stated that all the proceedings of the fair were to take place in the New Market ground and that if parties disobeyed the order the consequences would be serious. Another class of public notice stated that the fair and the statutes were to be holden as formerly at the top of Westgate, and in the streets, and in all particulars this latter form of notice was strictly attended to, and the statutes in consequence took place at the top of Westgate, and the streets were made to look busy and 'as of old'.

A detailed knowledge of what fair was on where and for how long was essential for any showman planning his annual route. This information was readily available in almanacs and similar publications but seasoned travellers would have had all the relevant details in their heads. This was certainly the case with the motley crowd of thieves, pickpockets and hangers-on who made their livings at these gatherings, as evidenced in a report by the Constabulary Commissioners in 1839:

> The Manchester youth questioned by the Commissioners knew the annual succession of fairs off by heart, and said that most thieves of his acquaintance could quote with equal accuracy. He had been round the circuit three times before reaching Salford Jail. [21]

The principal fairs and feasts in Old Wild's area, together with their dates, are shown on pp. 33–4. It should be noted that the actual date of a particular fair could vary quite considerably from year to year, especially in the case of those held at Easter and Whit, and these variations had to be taken into account when planning the yearly circuit. An early Easter, for example, meant that Wild's year started at Blackburn, while a late one would mean opening elsewhere (for instance, Bolton in 1849 and Accrington in 1859 [22]), and then moving on to Blackburn.

The dates being established, it had to be decided how far afield to travel and how many fairs to attend. Appendix A is a chronological chart of the journeyings of Old Wild's, and an examination of this evidence will show that in the earlier part of its life, up to the end of the 1840s, the show travelled farther than was the case from the 1850s onwards. Drypool, Hull, Knottingley, Manchester, Nottingham, Rotherham and Sheffield were all gradually omitted and the circuit became concentrated on a much

Details of Fairs and Feasts in the Region Travelled by Old Wild's (Listed Alphabetically)

Accrington	May 7. Fair.
Appleby	June 10, August 10. Fair.
Armley	September 4. Feast.
Ashton	March 23. Fair.
Barnsley	May 13, October 11. Fair.
Blackburn	Easter Monday for one week. Fair.
Bolton	January 4, July 30–31. Fair.
Bradford	June 17 (cattle), Dec. 9 (Statutes). Fair.
Bramley	July 19. Wakes.
Brighouse	August 17. Feast.
Burnley	March 6, July 10–11. Fair.
Bury	March 5, May 3, September 18. Fair.
Carlisle	Whitsun, Martinmas, August, September. Fair.
Colne	March 7, May 13, Oct. 11. Fair.
Dewsbury	Saturday on or before 25th July for one week. Feast
Drypool	c. 12th August. Feast.
Elland	July 9–11, Monday after August 12. Fair.
Halifax	24th June (horses & cattle), 1st Sat. in November (cattle).
Heckmondwike	Nov. 7. Fair.
Holbeck	Sept. 15. Feast.
Holmfirth	Beg. June and end October. Fair.
Horton	Beg. September. Feast.
Huddersfield	May 14th, October 4. Fair.
Hull	From October 11 for one week.
Hunslet	12th August. Feast.
Keighley	May 8th. Fair.
Kendal	Races last week in June. Fair May 22nd, November 8–9.
Knottingley	c. end July. Feast.
Lancaster	May 1st, July 5, October 10. Fair.
Leeds	July 10 (cattle), November 9th (Statutes).
Manchester	Easter Monday for one week (Knott Mill). Fair.

Nottingham	October 2 for 8 days. Goose Fair.
Penrith	Whit-Tuesday. Races 1st week in October.
Pontefract	May 5, October 5, November 30. Fair.
Preston	Whit Monday for 1 week. Pleasure fair.
Pudsey	23 August. Feast.
Ripon	1st Thursday and Friday in June. Feast.
Rochdale	May 14, November 7. Fair.
Sheffield	Whit-Tuesday for one week (cattle), 28th November (Statutes).
Skipton	March 24, Saturday after June 18. Fair.
Wakefield	4th July (cattle) and 11th November (Statutes).
Whitehaven	August 1. Fair.
Wigton	Day before and after June 27, October 28–30. Fair.
Wigton	20th February, 25th March, 5th April. Fair.

smaller area, roughly on a line between Preston and Leeds. The sketch plans on pp. 35 & 36 illustrate this point.

Part of the reduction in area travelled may lie in the development of Old Wild's itself. In the early years it was little more than a simple variety show, whereas by the late 1840s it was becoming one of the largest travelling theatres in the north of England. A small show with a limited programme would, of necessity, have to change location frequently in order to find new audiences. A prosperous portable theatre, on the other hand, especially with an extensive repertoire such as Wild's possessed, could stay in one place for a far longer period, changing the bill of fare daily. In this way the time spent and income lost in the weary round of dismantling, packing, travelling, unpacking and building up could be cut down considerably.

A reduction in the number of towns visited, therefore, would accord with the increasing prosperity of the company. The omission of Hull from the circuit, however, deserves some closer scrutiny since the evidence indicates that this had always been a particularly profitable location. The custom among showmen at that time (and, indeed, one that is followed to the present day) was to attend Nottingham Goose Fair for the eight days from October 2 and then pack up and make with all possible speed for Hull to be ready for the opening of the fair there on October 11. After 1841, Wild's was omitting Nottingham from its circuit

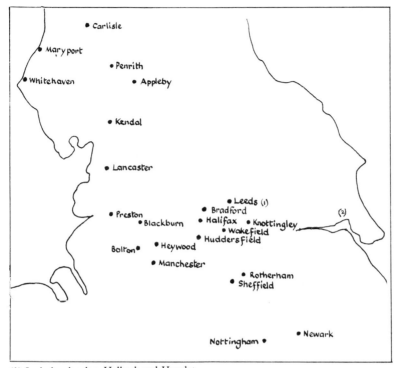

(1) Includes Armley, Holbeck and Hunslet
(2) Hull, Drypool, Beverley

Map 1
Locations visited by Wild's Theatre before 1850

and arriving in Hull by the beginning of October, usually remaining until
early November. This practice continued for several years, indicating
that the management were confident of good audiences in the seaport. In
addition, Sam Wild mentions appearing at a ball in Hull with 'Nelson',
which would appear to confirm the show's popularity there. Yet after
1847, Wild's never visited the town again [23].

The decision to drop Hull from the circuit may have been influenced
by an incident involving Sam which took place in 1847 but which, unlike
the ball, is not mentioned in his reminiscences. The *Hull Packet* of 15
October 1847, under the heading "Brother Showmen in Deadly
Conflict", records the details of a drunken brawl between Sam and Tom
Wild which resulted in Sam being bound over to keep the peace for
twelve months. Dependent as they were upon the goodwill of the local

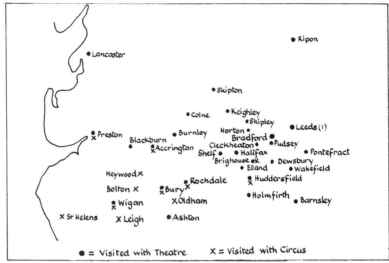

(1) Includes Armley, Holbeck and Hunslet

Map 2
Locations visited by Wild's Theatre and Circus post 1850

authorities to give them permission to remain in the town outside the official fair days, such an occurrence may well have been a deciding factor.

There had been another incident the previous year, at Beverley, a few miles further north. This took place just prior to Hull Fair and highlights the problems which could be experienced by a travelling theatre outside fairtime, and which could also have served to make the whole eastern part of the circuit less of an attractive proposition. The *Era* of 27 September 1846 reported:

> STROLLING PLAYERS. On Friday last, several of the respectable inhabitants of Beverley were greatly annoyed by a set of itinerant players coming into the town under the management of Mrs. Elizabeth Wild and her two sons, Thomas and Samuel Wild. Shortly after their arrival they commenced to erect a large booth in the Market Place, but in the course of the evening they were called upon by an inhabitant of the town and informed that if they acted, an information would be laid against them. In defiance, however, of this intimation they acted on Saturday evening. On Monday an information was laid against them, and the case was to have been

heard by the magistrates on Tuesday morning, but they, finding they had acted illegally, agreed to leave the town the following day, and the proceedings were abandoned.

The principal reason, however, must have been a geographical one and the omission of several towns from the route indicates that by the end of the 1840s more attention was being paid to the overall planning of an economical and profitable circuit. Two "average" circuits are shown below, one pre-, the other post-1850. These are based, not on specific years but rather on the towns and fairs known to have been on the circuit during those periods:

	Pre-1850			Post-1850	
Date	Location	Distance travelled	Date	Location	Distance travelled
Easter	Manchester		Easter	Blackburn	
Whit	Sheffield	c. 40 mls	Whit	Preston	c. 10 mls
June/	Halifax	35	June/	Halifax	42
July	Wakefield	18	July	Wakefield	18
	Leeds	11		Leeds	11
	Dewsbury	11		Dewsbury	11
Aug/	Knottingley	20	Aug/	Hunslet	10
Sept.	Drypool	40	Sept.	Armley	6
	Hunslet	60		Holbeck	6
	Armley	6	Oct.	Halifax	15
	Holbeck	6	Nov/	Dewsbury	12
Oct.	Hull	60	Dec.	Dewsbury	
Nov/Dec	Bradford	70			
Total mileage travelled in year:		373			137

The saving in overall mileage would seem sufficient reason in itself for omitting several towns from the yearly circuit. In addition, however, it was often the case that two or more major fairs were held at the same time and a choice had to be made as to which were likely to be more practical and profitable. Easter and Whit were popular fair dates in the north of England and while Manchester and Sheffield respectively were favoured by Wild's for these festivals before 1850, after that time they chose to play at Blackburn and Preston instead.

Sam makes little reference to Manchester in his recollections, but John Page, in his history of that city's fairs, recalls Wild's attending regularly up to the 1840s. As already noted, the Manchester city authorities were strongly opposed to these fairs, eventually succeeding in having them abolished in 1876. This does suggest that portable theatres wishing to perform in the city before or after the official fair days would have had difficulty in obtaining the necessary permission. At Blackburn, on the other hand, Wild's seldom had difficulty in gaining leave to play. It is certainly significant that by the 1870s, even before the fairs were abolished, portable theatres had become a rare sight in Manchester [24].

Prior to 1850 Old Wild's only recorded visit to Preston was for a winter season in Ryan's circus building in the 1830s. The Whit fair in that town was like Manchester's Knott Mill in that neither had been established by official charter. Preston's festivities had grown up around the custom of the workers and the country people assembling in the town on Whit Monday to make holiday and see their friends. In the 1830s few entertainments were provided for the crowds other than the processions of Friendly Societies, but by the beginning of the 1840s a few small shows began to attend. Gradually these began to grow in number until in the 1850s Preston Whit Fair was a major event in the local calendar, lasting for up to a week. Sam especially mentions the town as being one of the most profitable stops on the circuit during later years [25].

To substitute Blackburn and the increasingly popular Preston event for Manchester and Sheffield would therefore have been a practical decision, particularly when one takes into account the journey between the two latter towns. Even for a modern car this is a taxing mountain road: in the 1840s, for heavily-laden horse-drawn waggons it must have been a daunting undertaking. The road from Blackburn to Preston, on the other hand, has no such major obstacles to be tackled.

Gradually, then, the older, more widespread route was trimmed and shaped into an efficient and economical circuit, better suited to the prosperous travelling theatre that Old Wild's had become. On one occasion, however, a striking alteration was made to the usual pattern. In August 1849, Wild's set off on an extended tour of the Lake District, wintering in Carlisle and not returning to the "home ground" of Lancashire and Yorkshire until June of the following year [26]. This was a major deviation from the familiar areas and in view of the considerable distances involved (some 300 miles from leaving Leeds to returning to Preston), it is worth speculating on the motives which impelled it.

One reason may simply have been the desire to try new pastures. W. S. Thorne, who had started his career as a member of the Wild company, had been achieving some success in the towns of the north-east during the summer months of the 1830s and 40s while continuing to travel much the same circuit as Wild's the rest of the year [27]. Sam, who by this time was taking over the management from his mother, may have felt the urge to prove that his company could do just as well.

Two other factors may have influenced the decision. In 1848 Britain had suffered a severe depression in trade which was particularly felt in the industrial towns of Lancashire and Yorkshire. By 1849 the country was beginning to pull out of this recession, but if the previous year had been a bad one for the booth, the idea of trying a less industrialised area may have been attractive. There was also the threat of cholera. This disease, which had first reached Britain in the 1830s, reappeared in 1848, breaking out with renewed force in 1849. Naturally the areas worst affected were the overcrowded industrial towns where the death toll was very high [28]. In view of both the effect the epidemic might have on audiences and old Mrs. Wild's failing health, the Lake District may have seemed a wise choice. The experiment was not, however, repeated, Sam preferring the old familiar districts thereafter.

It will also be observed from Appendix A that from late 1861 up to 1865 (when the company was disbanded), Old Wild's made no visits whatever to Lancashire, although such towns as Blackburn, Burnley and Preston had been part of the circuit for many years. This may in part be due to Sam's failing fortunes which would make him unwilling to travel any further than absolutely necessary. A strong influencing factor, however, would have been the American Civil War which, by stopping the supply of raw materials to the Lancashire cotton towns, caused widespread hardship and distress. When the working people were on the verge of starvation they were unlikely to give a great deal of support to a travelling theatre, and as long as the cotton famine lasted, Sam would have seen little point in crossing the Pennines.

Within the circuit of industrial towns, Old Wild's seems to have had a particular affinity with Halifax. Sam's reminiscences frequently refer to his fondness for the place and the high regard in which the company was held there. This might be considered merely tactful, considering that his life story was being published in a Halifax newspaper, but in fact the evidence does seem to bear out his assertions. More visits are recorded for that town than for any other and there are many independent references to the show's popularity there. A report in the *Halifax Courier* of 30 June 1860 is typical:

> "Th' bottom o' th' market is'unt what it wor when I wor a lad", we heard a man say in a half querulous tone, himself at the time being in a sort of reverie. Did not Wild's theatrical establishment occupy the same well-known site, we should have completely agreed with him. . .

In view of this it is surprising that, as far as can be ascertained, Wild's never built a winter theatre in Halifax, although stays of up to two months were common, particularly after the autumn fair. One reason for this may be that the town already had an established theatre (which regularly objected to a licence being granted to the booth) [29]. It is likely that Sam, knowing his Halifax, was aware that whilst a licence for the booth would be fairly easy to obtain, the authorities would be less inclined to grant permission for a more permanent structure when there was already an established theatre in the town.

Overall, though, it is interesting to note how willingly licences were granted to Old Wild's, both for the booth and for winter buildings, despite opposition from other theatres and from religious groups. There are many instances of magistrates showing favour in this way: a particularly striking one was at Huddersfield in 1863. Samuel Pickles, a fellow showman, had applied for a licence to perform for the winter in a theatre he was having built in the market place. The magistrates suggested that he should complete the building and then re-apply for the licence so that they could judge of the theatre's suitability. In the meantime, Sam Wild applied for a similar licence. Both applications were eventually heard at the same time, and although Pickles should really have had the prior claim, a licence was granted only to Wild's, the authorities feeling that they could not grant two such licences for the same place. The main justification cited in favour of Wild's was that company's good reputation and blameless past, whereas it was said of Mr. Pickles that he had not always gone to the trouble of obtaining a licence where he performed [30].

This is a reminder that a good record was essential for any travelling company which habitually performed outside fairtime.

Wild's was always careful to emphasise its good reputation by frequent assurances, both in the press and on playbills, that disorderly conduct would be repressed and order enforced within the theatre. The management also took other steps to ensure that it would be welcomed when it applied for a licence, especially for the winter months. Stress was laid on the fact that the pieces presented would be those of the "better" authors such as Shakespeare, Lytton, etc. Another useful practice was to notify the authorities in advance that special benefit performances would be given in aid of local charities [31]. Sam mentions this custom as being an example of his family's generosity — as, indeed, to some extent it was. There is little doubt, however, that it was of considerable assistance to the company in obtaining both official sanction and public patronage (as well as a degree of extra publicity). Thus the *Era* of 7 November 1852, having noted that Wild's had donated five guineas to the Halifax Infirmary, observed: "The season. . . should have closed last week, but the manager was induced to take out a licence for one week longer". The same newspaper, on 20 January 1861, recorded of the company's winter sojourn at Blackburn:

> During the season Mr. Wild gave a benefit for the Infirmary, which yielded £5.5s for the Institution, being the first contribution to the local charities by any theatrical company. It is to be hoped that others will "go and do likewise". On Wednesday week the Proprietor gave a benefit to the Free Library. . . On account of the inclemency of the weather, the attendance was a failure, but notwithstanding this drawback, Mr. J. H. Williams, the Treasurer, handed over to the Free Library Committee in Mr. Wild's name 2 guineas.

Arthur Saxon describes the same custom being observed by Andrew Ducrow when touring England in the 1830s. Saxon goes further and states that the necessity of giving charity benefits was forced upon the travelling showman by the authorities in the towns which they visited [32]. There may well be some truth in this, but Old Wild's appears to have approached the practice in a more businesslike manner, goodwill on one side being exchanged for charitable donations on the other.

OLD WILD'S CIRCUIT IN THE YEAR 1857				
Dates	Location	Distance travelled	Time spent in location	Other details
Dec. '56 to Mar. '57 incl.	Dewsbury		c. 4 mths	Winter theatre.
April to mid-May	Blackburn	c. 50 mls	6 wks	Easter Fair started 13th April
Mid-May to mid-June	Preston	10	1 mth	Whitsun Fair started 1st June.
Mid-June to mid-July	Halifax	42	1 mth	Midsummer Fair started 24th June.
Mid-July to c. 21st July	Pontefract	32	1 wk	No fair known.
c. 24th July to 10th Aug.	Dewsbury	20	$2\frac{1}{2}$ wks	Feast held around 25th July.
c. 13th Aug. to 19th Aug.	Brighouse	15	1 wk	Feast held 17th August.
c. 21st Aug. to 28th Aug.	Pudsey	12	1 wk	Feast held 23rd August
Beg. Sept. to c. 10th Sept.	Armley	6	10 days	Feast held 4th Sept.
11th Sept. to end Sept.	Holbeck	6	3 wks	Feast held 15th Sept.
Beg. Oct.	Halifax	20	–	Licence delayed
Beg. Oct. to mid-Oct.	Dewsbury	18	2 wks	Winter theatre. Awaiting Halifax licence.
Mid-Oct. to mid-Dec.	Halifax	18	2 mths	Winter fair held c. beg. November.
Mid-Dec. to Mar. '58 incl.	Wigan	35	$3\frac{1}{2}$ mths	Theatre Royal.
Total Mileage Travelled:		284		

Information gathered principally from *The Era* but also from local newspapers and the text of *Old Wild's*.

Having looked at the overall pattern of the company's circuit, one year may now be looked at more closely. 1857 has been chosen as a year which is particularly well documented, and the chart on p. 42 details Old Wild's travels in that year.

Thirteen changes of location were made, the overall distance travelled being some 280 miles. The shortest journeys (those in the Pudsey-Armley-Holbeck area) would have taken about two hours each, based on an average 3 miles per hour, while the longest, Dewsbury to Blackburn, would probably have involved two days of travel with an overnight stop en route. The company's actions in October of that year are worth noting. When Sam Wild's application for a licence at Halifax was delayed, he moved his company to the Dewsbury theatre for a fortnight until the time came for his application to be re-heard (p. 156). This would have involved a day's journey in each direction but was obviously preferable to remaining idle for the intervening period. The incident illustrates both the increased efficiency and the greater prosperity of the company at this time: having a permanent theatre ready for such an emergency was an extremely useful asset.

Approximately one-third of that year was spent in a winter theatre. During the remainder, the time spent at each location varied from several days to a couple of months. Apart from Pontefract, all the visits coincided with local fairs, but on no occasion did the company confine itself to the official fair days alone.

The shortest period spent anywhere was a week and this is typical of Wild's circuit in the 1850s. As already noted, the larger a travelling theatre became the longer it could stay in one place and hence the less overall travelling it had to do. Among the longer stays, Halifax, Blackburn and Preston emerge as the most profitable locations, Halifax being visited twice with an overall total of three months being spent in the town, while at Blackburn and Preston the company stayed for six weeks and a month respectively.

Few travelling theatres took as much trouble as did Old Wild's to keep the public informed of their whereabouts through the pages of the *Era* and other publications. In consequence, information on the circuits of Wild's contemporaries is scanty. Some details, however, are available for those of Thorne, Wardhaugh and Purvis, and these are set out on p. [44].

William Thorne often competed with Wild's on the fairgrounds of

CIRCUITS OF OTHER TRAVELLING THEATRES [33]

(As information regarding actual dates is so sparse, the towns visited have been placed in alphabetical order)

Thorne 1832–54	Wardhaugh 1850's	Purvis 1832–33
Bilston	Altrincham	Alnwick
Bradford	Ashton	Bellingham
Bury	Barnsley	Berwick
Halifax	Brierley Hill	Darlington
Huddersfield	Burslem	Monkseaton
Hull	Burton-on-Trent	Newcastle
Kidderminster	Bury	Northallerton
Leeds	Congleton	Rothbury
N. Shields	Glossop	Stagshawbank
S. Shields	Hyde	Stockton
Sunderland	Lichfield	Tynemouth
Tunstall	Longton	Wooler
Tynemouth	Macclesfield	Yarm
Wakefield	Manchester	
York	Northwich	
	Rochdale	
	Stafford	
	Stalybridge	
	Stockport	

Yorkshire; Matthew Wardhaugh (who, like Thorne, had started his career with Wild's), kept mainly to the area of the Potteries, while Billy Purvis, during the period when he managed a theatrical company rather than a variety show, travelled the north-east and the Borders.

It will be seen that while both Wardhaugh and Purvis kept to their own particular regions, Thorne's circuit was more wide-ranging, taking in both of these areas and also a great deal of that covered by Wild's. A more detailed examination of the information available on Thorne's circuit, however, indicates that the journeys farther afield belong to the earlier years, c. 1832-49. After that time he concentrated on an area between Leeds and Kidderminster, following the same course of action as Wild's in trimming his circuit.

Where the real dividing line seems to have been drawn was between north and south. No record has been found of a northern booth visiting southern counties and only one in the reverse direction. William Green recounts the tale of a London showman who decided to try the northern fairs for a change and was looked upon as an intruder by the local folk who, as Green puts it, "stick to one location within a radius of fifty miles" [34]. He may have been exaggerating slightly, but all the evidence indicates that travelling theatres as a general rule kept to their own districts and did not cover the country overall.

It might be concluded that the difficulties of long-distance travel at that time would provide a simple explanation. This does not stand up, however, when the circuits of circuses are examined, since at the same period these shows were travelling throughout the length and breadth of Britain and beyond. In 1843, for example, Batty's visited Dublin, Jersey and Leicester within the space of a few months, while in 1845 Hughes' was at Dublin in August and Ely in September. Sanger's, which visited every part of the British Isles in the 1850s, was touring the Continent each summer by the 1870s, returning to England for the winter [35].

A possible explanation for this striking difference in circuit pattern is that circuses travelled more widely because they were able to do so: the very nature of the entertainment they presented made it acceptable over a far wider area. It is feasible to postulate that booth theatres, relying on the spoken word, would experience some difficulty in coping with regional accents and dialects. In addition, plays that went down well in, say, industrial Yorkshire, might not appeal in a Sussex farming village. Circuses, on the other hand, relying on mainly visual displays of feats of dexterity and horsemanship, would have no problems of communication. Some substance is given to this theory by the anonymous actress who travelled with Wild's in the 1850s. She confirmed that Sam was much admired in his home area,

. . .but twice he went further afield, and found himself completely out of his latitude, his takings being so inconsiderable that he hastily retreated on both occasions to his old quarters, and his motto ever since has been, "Never no more out o' sight o' them big chimneys". [36]

With hindsight, the next obvious step from such a concentrated circuit was to establish permanent theatres in the most profitable towns.

Purvis, Thorne, Wardhaugh and Wild all built permanent or semi-permanent theatres, but only Wardhaugh prospered enough to make the final step of staying put for good. Ill-health overtook both Purvis and Thorne, and an ill-advised circus experiment by Sam Wild cost him both his savings and his confidence [37]. It does not seem likely, on the other hand, that Sam would ever have given up the travelling life completely. There were many occasions during the prosperous years when he could have made a move towards doing so by leaving the booth and transferring his company from one to another of the winter buildings which he had erected in different towns. No matter how long his winter season in one of these, however, he always returned to the booth. He had, after all, been born into the travelling life and it was the only existence he really understood. Even in the late 1860s, poverty-stricken and in failing health, he still made many attempts to start up the business again, refusing to believe that the heyday of the travelling theatre was already over (pp. 238–9).

REFERENCES

1.   28 Geo. III, c. lxviii, 6 & 7 Vic., c. lxviii.
2.   Addison, W., *The Old Roads of England*, 1980, 123.
3.   Arthur, T., *The Life of Billy Purvis*, 1875, 88.
4.   Sanger Coleman, G., *The Sanger Story*, 1956, 19.
5.   Fenwick, A. J., *Travelling Shows* (MS), 1939, Fenwick Collection, Newcastle-upon-Tyne.
6.   O.W. 101–2.
7.   Mayhew, H., *op. cit.*, 130.
8.   O.W. 40, 89, 221, 153; *Era* 9.7.1843; O.W. 172 & *Oxberry's Budget* 5.2.1844.
9.   *Halifax Express*, 22.12.1838; *Preston Pilot*, 13.6.1840; *Leeds Mercury*, 13.11.1841.
10.   Miller, D. P., *op. cit.*, 46–7.
11.   Muncey, R. W., *Our Old English Fairs*, 1935, 159; *Hull Advertiser*, 18.10.1839.
12.   O.W. 174; Page, J., *Manchester Fairs*, M'cr Lit. Club Papers, 1877.
13.   Arthur, T., *op. cit.*, 108.
14.   Sanger, G., *Seventy Years a Showman*, first pub. 1910, this ed. 1927, 45.
15.   O.W. 100; playbill collections and local newspapers at Bradford, Hull, Preston and Wakefield.
16.   See for example, Miller, D. P., *op. cit.*, 44–45.
17.   *Preston Guardian*, 5.6.1852.
18.   Braithwaite, D., *Fairground Architecture*, 1968, 37. *Preston Herald* 29.5.1858.
19.   Willson Disher, M., *Fairs, Circuses and Music Halls*, 1942, 30.
20.   Cunningham, H., "The Metropolitan Fairs" *in* Donajgrodski, A. P. (ed.) *Social Control in Nineteenth Century Britain*, 1977, 168–72. Information supplied by Manchester Central Library Local History Dept. *Halifax Guardian*, 30.6.1855; O.W. 82.

21. Quoted in Dallas, D., *The Travelling People*, 1971, 12.
22. O.W. 79; *Era*, 10.4.1859.
23. Playbill collection, Hull Central Library; O.W. 78.
24. Page, J., *op. cit.*
25. O.W. 39: local newspapers, Harris Library, Preston; O.W. 132.
26. O.W. 82–83 & local newspapers, Kendal, Lancaster, Penrith.
27. O.W. 21; King, R., *North Shields Theatres*, 1948, 130 ff.
28. Longmate, N., *King Cholera*, 1966.
29. Local newspapers, Halifax Central Library.
30. *Halifax Courier*, 6.12.1862.
31. Playbill collections, Bradford, Hull & Wakefield Central Libraries.
32. Saxon, A. H., "The Tyranny of Charity" in *Nineteenth Century Theatre Research*, Vol. I, No. 2, 1973, 95–106.
33. *Thorne's circuit*: *Era*; also King, R., *op. cit.*: playbill collection, North Shields Ref. Library. *Wardhaugh's circuit*: Slater, T., *Reminiscences of an Actor's Life*, 1892. *Purvis's circuit*: Arthur, T., *op. cit.*
34. Green, W., *op. cit.*, 280.
35. *Era* & Sanger Coleman, G., *op. cit.*, 17.
36. *Chambers' Journal*, *op. cit.*
37. *Era*; Slater, T., *op. cit.*, Arthur, T., *op. cit.*; O.W. 189–195.

CHAPTER 3

THE AUDIENCE

In the past most studies of the Victorian theatre and its audience have tended to concentrate on London and to make assumptions for the country as a whole based on those for the metropolis. Happily this pattern is now starting to change: Kathleen Barker's detailed work on Bristol is an encouraging example of the new trend as are Jeremy Crump's study of the Theatre Royal Leicester and that of Douglas Reid for Birmingham [1]. All too many researchers, though, still seem to take it for granted that findings for London must apply to all of Britain. Typical is Gilbert Cross's statement in his purportedly general study of melodrama:

> No study of nineteenth century domestic melodrama would be valid without an examination of its audience. It is, therefore, upon the London audience that attention must now be focused. [2]

The selection of London for close study may be understandable in view of the greater amount of available data, but it can hardly be regarded as representing the overall picture of Victorian theatregoing. The shaping force of the nineteenth century was the Industrial Revolution and the main effects of that revolution were felt not in London but in the northern half of England where villages mushroomed into cities and populations multiplied at a speed hitherto unknown. As had been seen in the previous chapter, Old Wild's circuit lay almost exclusively within these heavily industrialised areas with their new populations, hungry for entertainment; a study of its audience, therefore, is of considerable importance in assembling the full picture of nineteenth-century playgoing in England. For the purposes of discussion, the audience in the booth and in the winter theatre are taken to be broadly similar, although, where relevant, differences will be noted. For various reasons the audience during fairtime is likely to have differed materially from that at other times, and will be discussed separately.

The first step in establishing the kind of people who made up the audience at Wild's is to look at the towns on the circuit and their populations. They may be divided into two categories: those which had been established centres of population before the Industrial Revolution and those which came into being as a direct result of industrialisation. Among the former may be listed Hull, Leeds and Preston, all of which had been of some importance in the previous century. Preston, for example, had in the 1790s been considered the social centre of Lancashire with "a theatre, assembly room, coffee and newsrooms, a book club, a race course and open spaces in which one could promenade" [3]. The population at that time was a blend of social classes: the Earl of Derby had a mansion there and well-to-do members of the local squirearchy also lived in or close to the town, in fairly close proximity to the poorer inhabitants.

As more and more factories were built in these older towns, and as the housing for the workers began to fill up every vacant space, the middle and upper classes moved outside to where the air was still clean and conditions less crowded. This movement was general throughout Lancashire and Yorkshire in the 1830s and 40s. In 1844, Engels, writing of central Manchester, observed

> . . .the absence of the higher classes, who, like the aristocracy, do not live in the town. The town, strictly speaking. . . is only inhabited by shopkeepers and operatives; the merchants and manufacturers have detached villas in the midst of gardens and parks in the country. [4]

By the 1850s even the shopkeepers were leaving the town centres. A General Board of Health Enquiry at Halifax in 1850 heard evidence which showed that tradesmen of that town were transferring their families to the suburbs. [5]

As those who could afford to do so moved out, the towns became almost entirely working class. A survey carried out at Manchester as early as 1836 found that 64% of the total population was within this social group, and a similar study at Leeds in 1839 estimated the labouring population to be about 75% of the total figure for the town [6].

The second category of towns — those which came into being as a direct result of industrialisation — were generally outlying districts of older urban settlements. In the early days, when power was still provided by fast-moving water, mills had to be located where this source of energy could be found. The older towns, usually situated in a valley, were not suitable. Hence the growth of such places as Armley, Holbeck and Hunslet around Leeds and the ring of satellite towns around Manchester: all close enough to the major centre to enable the goods produced to be dealt with through the commercial channels there. With the advent of steam, factories began to be built in the older towns themselves, but the satellite towns remained although their rate of growth slowed.

As might be expected, the population of these satellite towns was almost exclusively working class. Engels remarked of the towns around Manchester that they were "purely industrial. . . inhabited only by working men and petty tradesmen" and indeed the statistics for Bury show that 75 % of the inhabitants were working class in 1836. A committee sitting at Leeds in 1839 described Holbeck and Hunslet as forming together "a densely populated working class area" and Asa Briggs suggests that these two out-townships had

> much the same kind of reputation as the *faubourgs* of medieval cities where artisans who could not find or could not afford accommodation within the city lived and worked. [7]

The population within the towns on the Wild circuit was therefore almost entirely of this order. Within that general classification, however, there were wide differences in earning capacity and social status which materially affected people's ability to patronise the theatre with any regularity.

At the bottom of the scale, both financially and socially, were the unfortunate handloom weavers, many thousands of whom were still living in the industrial towns at this time. From being the élite and the highest-paid of all workers at the beginning of the century, earning 30s to 35s a week or more, they had descended, victims of the new machinery, to a penny an hour in the 1830s and 40s [8]. Barely able to survive, they had nothing to spare for luxuries like entertainment. In any industrial town there were also innumerable small industries and sweatshops which serviced the huge factories and their workers; the employees in these smaller concerns were badly paid, often on a piecework basis, which meant working as many hours as they were able, in order to scrape a living.

Domestic service was still the largest single employer of women and the second largest employer overall throughout the nineteenth century [9]. In the industrial towns, however, the wages offered and the discipline imposed did not encourage many to opt for this kind of work and the new suburbanites found it difficult to obtain the staff appropriate to their status. Those who did enter domestic service had virtually no free time of their own and received very low wages which, even if leisure time had been available, would not have permitted frequent visits to the theatre. As one contemporary observer put it:

> Wages for female domestics vary from £8 to £20 per annum. . . [and] fail to tempt girls from the associations of factory life, with its evenings of freedom for visits and gossip. [10]

Much has been written of the hardships and evils of factory work in the last century but it has not perhaps been fully recognised that when compared to other, more traditional, forms of employment, many saw it as relatively pleasant and well paid. In cases where the whole family was so employed, quite a high income could be generated. A survey of 1860 assessed the earnings of workers over the previous twenty years and concluded that the families of factory hands in Lancashire were "at present earning higher incomes than many of the professional classes". It went on to state:

> Similar high rates of wages prevail throughout Yorkshire and the other manufacturing districts where women and children also largely contribute to increase the united earnings of families. [11]

There was also a new social phenomenon, brought about by the need for large numbers of younger people in factory work. This was the increasing number of boys and girls becoming self-sufficient and leaving home to set up for themselves at an earlier age than would have been possible in pre-industrial times. Disraeli comments on this practice in *Sybil*, and a Parliamentary enquiry of the same period notes that while younger children handed most of their earnings to their parents, by the age of fourteen or so, "many of them begin to have strong desires for finer clothing or for other things, and they frequently stipulate with their parents for some portion of their wages" [12]. Mary Bayly, whose study

Lancashire Homes and What Ails Them appeared in 1863, observed:

> Girls of fourteen and fifteen leave their homes, pay sixpence a week
> for lodging. . . The streets are filled of an evening with gaily-dressed
> girls and idle, smoking lads. . . I stood before about a hundred of
> these young girls and asked if all who were living at home with their
> parents would hold up their hands. Not one quarter of the hands
> went up. [13]

There was, therefore, a considerable percentage of the population, both
male and female, in any industrial town which was young, free of family
commitments and financially independent. There is a point here worth
emphasising: for perhaps the first time women were free to choose where
to go and how to live, being able to pay for themselves instead of having
to rely on men's support.

The admission charges at Old Wild's remained fairly constant
throughout its existence at 1s, 6d and 3d. When compared with the prices
at established theatres in the region during the same period, the latter are
found to be considerably higher. At Hull Theatre Royal in the 1840s, the
range was from 3s for a box seat to 1s in the upper gallery. Half price at
9 p.m. brought the cheapest seats to 6d. At Wakefield around the same
time the lowest-priced seats were 6d with no second price. Admission
prices at Blackburn's major theatre in the 1850s were comparatively high
at 2s and 1s6d, while at Halifax, the most frequently-visited town on the
Wild circuit, seats at the Theatre Royal in the 1860s ranged from 2s6d
to 6d. [14]

Wild's was therefore less expensive than a major theatre. It was not,
however, the cheapest theatrical entertainment available: most of the
larger industrial areas supported two or three penny gaffs which catered
for the poorest — or, as one report censoriously expressed it, "the very
lowest elements" — in society [15].

The timing of performances at Old Wild's should also be taken into
account. At this period the custom in major theatres was for performances
to commence around 7 p.m. and finish around midnight. This would have
made it impossible for factory employees, who seldom got out before 8,
to attend shows from the beginning, and indeed some acknowledgement
of this was made in the provision of half-price seats at 9 p.m. At Wild's,
however, performances started at 8 and finished around 10.30. This made

Plate 5. Children peeking through the canvas at the back of a fairground booth (cf p. (57)). Reproduced from Pierce Egan's *Life of an Actor* (1825). *Collection of George Speaight.*

WILD'S THEATRE,
HOP-YARD, HOWDEN.

HOLLO! STOP & READ
The long looked for come at last.

One of the greatest Treats ever offered to the Public of Howden and the surrounding Neighbourhood.

FIRST NIGHT OF THE

COMIC PANTOMIME
OF
THE ICE WITCH
With New Scenery, Tricks, and Transformation.

On MONDAY Evening, September 19th, 1859
The performance will commence with the Romantic Drama, entitled the

IDIOT WITNESS
Or, A TALE OF BLOOD.

Le Sœur Arnaud ... Mr J. B. KEEFE.　Robert Arnaud, (his Son)... Mr SMITH.　Paul Tugwell, (a Ferryman)... Mr R. HEWITT
Hans Gerthold ... Mr R. PATON.　Walter Arlington, (Page to the Queen)... Mr MACGUINNESS.
Earl of Sussex ... Mr DELAFIELD,　Gilbert, (the Idiot Witness)... Mr J. C. DONNELLY
Dame Tugwell ... Mrs FRANCE.　Janet, (her Daughter) ... Mrs MACGUINNESS.

Song　-　-　-　-　-　Mr HEWITT.

To conclude with, for the first time in this Town, with entire New Scenery painted for the occasion, Tricks, Mechanical Changes, New and Original, Serious—Artistical—Bombastical—Comical—Dogmatical—Emblematical—Fantastical—Geographical—Hyperbolical—Intrinsical—Jestical—Kaleidescopal—Lyrical—Mystical—Nonsensical—Orthodoxical—Paradoxical—Quizzical—Raphsodical—Systematical—Terpsichordical—Unsophistical—Ventriloquistical—Whimsical—Y'cleptical—Zoetical

COMIC PANTOMIME ENTITLED THE

ICE WITCH
Or, HAROLD OF THE FROZEN HAND.

Harold of the Frozen Hand ... Mr MACGUINNESS.　Magnus Snorö, his henchman ... Mr J. C. DONNELLY
Sweno, a Norwegian Chief ... Mr PATON.　Gruthiof, chief demon of the hills ... Mr J. B. KEEFE.

Sterno	Demons attendant upon Gruthiof	Mr R. HEWITT	Atcho	Mr SMITH
Hacho		Mr CARR.	Keepo	Demons attendant upon Gruthiof	Mr HOLLAND
Kilbo		Mr DELAFIELD	Sleepo		Mr WILSON.

Druda, the Ice Witch ... Mrs MACGUINNESS.　Lady Ulla ... Mrs POWELL
Minna, her attendant ... Mrs FRANCE.

FAIRIES.

Heela, chief of the Fairies ... Mrs J. C. DONNELLY.　Hilda ... Mrs R. HEWITT.　Freyer, the Sun God ... Miss WILD
Puckle ... Mrs SMITH.　Audanto ... Mrs POWELL.

Scenery and incidents connected with the opening—View of the Frozen Sea and Icebergs by Moonlight—Wreck of Harold's Ship—Chorus of Ice Spirits—Sudden appearance of Druda upon her Ice Chariot—her interview with Harold—Splendid Mechanical Change—Grand Fairy Lake and Coral Grotto—Song by Druda—PICTURE.
VIEW—Magic Letter and Ludicrous Situation of Magnus and his Fairy Sweetheart—Hall in Sweno's Castle—Lady Ulla and Minna borne away by Gruthiof and his demons.
The Frozen Regions—the False Lover—the Ice Witch's Farewell to the Traitor Harold—the Frozen Hand, and his departure—Chorus. Magic Cavern of Gruthiof, the Demon King—Sudden and Splendid Appearance of Freyer, the Sun God, who Vows to protect the Innocent —Tower and Battlements of Gruthiof's Castle—Arrival of Harold—Desperate Encounter with the Demons.

GRAND TRANSFORMATION, and now the Fun begins.

Runzonefunnycomecomeallhogetheroufromtomestall, afterwards clown ... Mr CARR,　Spiderlimb, afterwards Pantaloon ... Mr HEWITT
Harlequine ... Mr SMITH.　Columbine ... Mrs POWELL.

On TUESDAY Evening, Sept. 20th,
The performance will commence with the Powerful Drama, entitled the

CHARCOAL BURNER
Or, The DROPPING WELL of KNARESBOROUGH.

Godfrey Harrington ... Mr J. B. KEEFE.　Matthew Eadale, (a Miser) ... Mr PATON　Edmund Esdale ... Mr SMITH
Poynet Arden, (the Reckless, known as the Charcoal Burner of Aidwood Priory) ... Mr MACGUINNESS.
Mr Valentine Verdict ... Mr R. HEWITT.　Caleb Brown ... Mr DELAFIELD.　Abel Cole ... Mr CARR
Edith Harrington, (the Fair Maid of York betrothed to Edmund Esdale) ... Mrs MACGUINNESS.
Barbara Jones, (her waiting Maid) ... Mrs FRANCE.　Old Mother Grumble ... Mrs SMITH.

Song　-　-　-　-　-　Mr CARR.

To conclude with for the second time the Comic Pantomime of the

ICE WITCH.

Stage Manager, Mr Donnelly.　Prompter, Mr Keefe.　Leader of the Orchestra, Mr Scott
Doors open at Seven, Performances commence at Half-past.
BOXES, ONE SHILLING　PIT, SIXPENCE　GALLERY THREEPENCE
Police Officers will be in attendance to keep order.　Smoking strictly prohibited.　No admittance behind the Scenes.

WILLIAM SMALL, PRINTER, HOWDEN.

Plate 8.
Nautical and dog dramas on the same bill at Holbeck in 1859. *Reproduced by courtesy of West Yorkshire Archive Service, Bradford.*

it feasible for workers to get there in time for curtain-up; and it is significant that Sam Wild refers to opening the doors early, providing pre-show music and keeping warm fires in winter [16]. To the tired operative coming out of the factory gates in the evening, the attraction of the welcoming and comfortable booth must have been well nigh irresistible. The earlier hour of finishing, too, would have been in the booth's favour since workers could not afford to stay up late — as W. A. Abram observed:

> The early and strict hours of labour at the mill compel the work people to a-bed early and after eleven o'clock at night the absolute quietude of a manufacturing town is in strange contrast with the midnight din of London and Liverpool. [17]

From the foregoing evidence a clearer picture begins to emerge. The factory workers were the social group most able to frequent the theatre and the fact that Old Wild's circuit rarely went outside the industrial towns establishes beyond doubt that this was the audience at which it was aiming. The gallery, the largest single area of seating in the booth, was the province of the younger workers, both male and female; and it is not surprising that it is frequently mentioned as a source of disturbance. It is quite likely that young women outnumbered young men; significantly, after a gallery collapse at Keighley in 1859, most of the items found were articles of female finery — "shawls, bonnets, boas", etc. This parallels the evidence for audience composition at major theatres of the period where the gallery always provided the biggest and most regular audience. [18]

The pit, a much smaller seating area, would have been occupied by older factory workers and couples; in seaport towns, sailors home on leave attended, and Sam mentions the captains of the boats which plied up and down the Humber being regular patrons (p. 101). With regard to the boxes there is likely to have been some difference between the booth and the winter theatre. As noted in Chapter 1, although box seating was provided in both, greater capacity was allowed in the winter building and on at least one occasion a particularly large box was installed, holding 40 or more.

Box seats were normally occupied by those whom Sam delighted to call "distinguished patrons". In his memoirs he makes much of visits by the aristocracy (the Marquis of Douro, Sir George Musgrave, etc.) but in fact such occasions were few. Most of them, in fact, took place during Wild's one tour of the Lake District in 1849 and probably reflect the still surviving tradition there of the squirearchy supporting and patronising strolling players. More usual was the patronage of societies like the Ancient Order of Foresters or the Royal Order of Buffaloes. Sam Wild was a member of the former society for most of his life and this would have assisted his claim for their patronage. Other booth managers also realised the advantages of such membership: Jones, with whom Sam and the young Wallett appeared at Hull in the 1830s (p. 26), advertised himself as "Brother Jones" on playbills announcing patronage by the Society of Oddfellows, and assured those attending that they would be shown to their seats by "another Brother of the Society" [19].

A locally stationed regiment could also be a useful source of patronage. At Bradford in 1844, for example, the 17th Regiment not only attended in force but also provided some "military amateurs" for the leading roles in *The Ostler and the Robber* (a useful device for ensuring support). At Burnley in 1858 the presence of Capt. J. G. Irvine and the officers of the 71st Regiment of Light Infantry at the winter theatre explains the construction of the 40-seater box; a special sectioned-off area where the whole group could sit together is likely to have appealed as much to those in command as to the men themselves [20].

It is probable that the winter theatre had a slightly more "up market" audience than did the booth with its atmosphere of the fairground and unconventional travelling life. Two pieces of evidence support this premise. The first, which will be discussed in more detail in Chapter 4, is that Shakespeare, rarely presented during summer seasons, featured prominently in the winter programmes. The second is that while advertising for the booth was by means of playbills distributed to shops, homes and places of work, considerable use was also made in winter of local newspapers, indicating a potential audience which habitually read these publications. The evidence also suggests that for many theatregoing was a regular habit, some attending several nights a week. Sam records particular groups of "gallery-ites" visiting them at Bradford every night in the 1840s (pp. 67–69), and on at least one occasion season tickets were issued for pit and boxes [21].

The booth audience during fairtime is likely to have been somewhat different. In the first place, the whole town was on holiday on these festive occasions and there was a strong tradition of saving up for the fair and spending every penny on merrymaking. To the factory workers, therefore, were added all those who during the rest of the year could not spare even one hour from their desperate fight to earn a living but who, on this special day, emerged into the unfamiliar daylight determined to enjoy themselves. Even maidservants and scullery lads, particularly if it was a hiring fair, had one day free from household tyranny before the necessity of seeking a new place was forced upon them.

In addition it was the custom for large numbers of country people to visit the town at fairtime. In earlier years, when trading was still the most important aspect of the fair, rural visitors used the occasion to sell their own produce and buy household necessities. Other events of a more important nature were also timed to fit in with the annual festival. The *Hull Advertiser* of 15 October 1808 recorded:

> On Tuesday last, being the Fair Day, there were thirty-nine christenings at the Holy Trinity Church at this place.

A railway worker of the 1840s affirmed the importance of the occasion when he recollected, "We settled to be married next Fair Day — and so we were". [22]

The trading aspect became less important from the 1820s onward but the pleasure fair grew and became the main attraction. The flow of visitors from outlying areas increased rather than decreased as the century wore on — a fact remarked upon by many local newspapers. The *Bradford Observer* of 21 June 1838 observed:

> The pleasure fair began on Saturday, when the influx of country people was very great, and we should think the show folk did best on that evening. . .

By now, however, instead of farmers and their wives, it was the younger rural dwellers who came to see the sights: there are frequent patronising references in the newspaper reports to "simple swains" and "country bumpkins". [23]

The development of the railways also helped to swell the numbers of fairgoers coming in from other towns to join in the fun. The *Hull Packet* of 15 October 1847 reported that the fair had been "more numerously attended than in any previous year", the trains being "crowded to excess". The same newspaper, a a year later, noted that steamers had been used to ferry pleasure-seekers across the Humber from the Manchester, Sheffield and Lincolnshire railway. The *Preston Pilot* of 5 June 1852 observed:

> The arrival of strangers during the day was immense, trains being put on at very low fares from Lancaster, Carlisle, Blackburn and all the neighbouring towns.

Children as might be expected, formed a large part of the fairground crowd. An interesting fact, however, is that middle-class children were often allowed to attend the annual fair as a treat, despite the considerable opposition by this social group to fairs generally, as noted in Chapter 2. Many autobiographical sketches — among them those of Sam Wild's recorder, William Broadley Megson (pp. 7–9) — testify to the importance of this yearly event in childhood's calendar. One writer in the *Preston Pilot* of 5 June 1852 lamented nostalgically:

> We never see the brown canvass [*sic*] of shows and booths in a fair or other great gathering together of pleasure-seeking folk without regretting that our years of round jackets are for ever flown.

An article in the *Halifax Courier* dated 29 June 1878 has a similar tone:

> Writing these words recalls to memory a happy time when to childish fancy Halifax Fair was the one great carnival of the year. A quiet day was to be chosen for the visit — certainly not the 24th, when dangers beset every street corner, because of wayward horses and obstinate bulls — nor yet Great Saturday when the crowd of country cousins crammed the fairground to suffocation. No, it must be the second or third day of the Fair, and one and all must be there as soon after noon as the donning of clean frocks and collars would permit. And the wealth one's pockets contained!. .... And then, at the Fair, with the grand shows, chief among them Wild's at the bottom of the Market!

The happy memories of one such child were to aid Old Wild's in a practical way in later years. When Sam was having some difficulty obtaining a licence at Halifax in 1857, one Colonel Pollard remembered the show "where we used to pay our pennies to see the fortune-telling pony" and gave his approval (p. 157).

The fairground crowd, therefore, was a mixed one, town dwellers mingling with visitors from both the country and other towns, and children very much in evidence (although working-class children certainly outnumbered those from the middle class). There would also have been a sprinkling of reporters, interested observers and middle-class parents. It does not necessarily follow, however, that all these groups would have been represented equally in the audience at Old Wild's. As noted in Chapter 2, there were many shows on the fairground and the travelling theatre was one of the most expensive. (This, incidentally, was still true to the very last days of portable theatres. One old lady, recollecting Stalybridge Wakes in the early years of this century, told me that as children they could never afford the admission charges to the fairground theatres and had to try and wriggle in under the canvas at the back).

While the country folk from remoter areas, where a travelling theatre was a novelty, were eager to visit the booth, and better-off workers were out to spend their savings and enjoy themselves, Wild's admission charges of 6d and 3d would have been out of reach of those with limited resources. Many smaller shows only charged a penny, while hand-propelled roundabout rides might only cost a halfpenny (if you were strong and enthusiastic, you could even get a free ride in return for pushing the roundabout once or twice) [24]. The likelihood is, therefore, that poorer workers and children, to whom even 3d would have represented an enormous sum, would not have formed a very large proportion of the audience. There is no evidence, incidentally, that children were ever admitted at a reduced rate at Wild's and on occasion a positive embargo was laid on infants in arms [25]. There is little doubt, however, that the portable theatres held an enormous fascination for the rising generation, and while they might not always have been able to raise the necessary capital, there are many references to the crowds of children that clustered around the outside parade, enjoying the free show that preceded each performance. Then, as Sam's biographer puts it, "having advanced in years just a little", and having improved their worldly circumstances, they too were able to mount the magical steps and enter the glittering world of make-believe.

REFERENCES

1. Barker, K., *Bristol at Play*, 1976; Thirty Years of Struggle: Entertainment in Provincial Towns 1840–1870 *in Theatre Notebook* Vol. XXXIX, 1985, Nos. 1–3. Crump, J., "A Study of the Theatre Royal, Leicester, 1847–1900" *in Theatre Notebook* Vol. XXXVIII, 1984, No. 2. Reid, D. A., "Popular Theatre in Victorian Birmingham" *in* Bradby, D., James, L., and Sharratt, B. (eds) *Performance and Politics in Popular Drama*, 1980.
2. Cross, G., *Next Week East Lynne*, 1977, 67.
3. Marshall, J. D., *Lancashire* in the *City & County Histories* series, 1974, 56.
4. Engels, F., *The Condition of the Working Classes in England*, first pub. 1845, first British ed. 1892.
5. Parker, V., *The English House in the 19th Century*, 1970, 22.
6. Manchester Statistical Society, *Report on the Condition of the Working Classes*, 1834, 1835, 1836. Harrison, J., *Early Victorian Britain*, 1980, 83.
7. Briggs, A., *Victorian Cities*, 1963, 27.
8. Longmate, N., *Milestones in Working Class History*, 1975.
9. Burnett, J. (ed.), *Useful Toil*, 1974, 135.
10. Quoted in Longmate, N., *The Hungry Mills*, 1978, 45.
11. Quoted in Burnett, J., *op. cit.*
12. Disraeli, B., *Sybil: or. The Two Nations*, 1845. PP 1833 xx D2 17. Quoted in Anderson, M., *Family Structure in 19th Century Lancashire*, 1971.
13. Quoted in Longmate, N., *The Hungry Mills*, 49.
14. Playbill collections, relevant towns; also local newspapers.
15. *Manchester Guardian.* 20.3.1830.
16. Playbill collections, Bradford & Hull; also O.W. 28.
17. Abram, W. A., "Social Condition and Political Prospects of the Lancashire Workman" *in The Fortnightly Review*, Oct. 1868.
18. O.W. 67–69, 160, 186; *Halifax Guardian* 21.12.1850.
19. Playbill dated Oct. 1840, playbill collection Hull.
20. O.W. 66, 166–167.
21. *Bury Advertising Gazette*, 1.12.1853.
22. Quoted in Burnett, J. *op. cit.*
23. Local newspapers, Bradford, Hull, Preston.
24. *Preston Herald*, 29.5.1858.

CHAPTER 4

THE REPERTOIRE OF OLD WILD'S

The repertoire of a nineteenth-century travelling theatre is of considerable interest, reflecting as it must both the capabilities of the company and the tastes of its audience. Sam Wild's memoirs make reference to some 120 pieces performed over a period of about forty years; research has brought this number to over 300, details of which will be found in Appendix B.

It is not possible to be precise about the size of any booth's repertoire, owing to the frequency with which the same pieces were presented under alternative and sometimes misleading titles. Sam Wild admits that in the company's declining years he sometimes indulged in the practice of altering titles in order to make an old play seem like a new one (p. 222). The evidence, in fact, indicates that this was the norm throughout the booth's life. At Hull in 1842, for example, a "thrilling nautical melodrama" was brought out, entitled *Bound 'Prentice to a Waterman*. In the same town a year later the play was again presented but this time as "a beautiful romantic drama" called *The Law of Java*. The fact that A. V. Campbell is the author ascribed by Allardyce Nicoll to the former piece and George Colman the Younger to the latter, whereas the cast lists are identical (e.g. Artoise Latour the Death Dealer, Dick Dark a Waterman, who certainly do not appear in Colman's piece), gives some indication of the problems involved in assigning a collection of nineteenth-century drama titles. In many cases only an examination of surviving playbills has made identification possible. *The Broken-Hearted Father* and *Smiles and Tears*, for example, were both found to be versions of W. T. Moncrieff's *The Lear of Private Life*, and the list of characters in *Wilfrid Clitheroe: or, The Husband of Two Wives* indicates that this is in fact T. E. Wilks' *Kate Wynsley, Cottage Girl* [1].

It should be emphasised, too, that Appendix B cannot claim to represent anything like a complete list of the plays performed by Old Wild's during the forty years of its life as a travelling theatre. The information obtained is sparse and widely scattered; yet, incomplete as it is, it provides such a larger number of titles that it is reasonable to assume the true figure as being considerably higher. The titles that have been recorded, however, being representative of various periods throughout that forty years, may be taken as a sample on which to base some general conclusions.

A glance at Appendix B shows a considerable variety in the repertoire of Old Wild's. "The standard plays of Shakespeare [*sic*], Knowles, Bulwer, and other popular authors" claimed by Sam certainly appear, but so do war spectacles, dog dramas, nautical pieces, pantomimes, burlesques, comic ballets and farces, together with a great number of the popular melodramas of the day. A survey of the most frequently-occurring authors gives the following "top five":

C. R. Somerset	14 titles recorded
J. B. Buckstone	13
E. Fitzball	10
J. T. Haines	10
Shakespeare	10

No other author is represented more than seven times. These results show, predictably, a strong bias in favour of the popular melodramatists. Shakespeare's inclusion, however, is worth noting and will be discussed later.

When we come to look at those plays for which performances are most frequently recorded, the picture is a little different. Of all known performances by the company, the following titles appear most frequently:

Mungo Park	(Bernard)	26 performances recorded
Hamlet	(Shakespeare)	16
The Pirate Ship	(Somerset)	16
Macbeth	(Shakespeare)	15
Othello	(Shakespeare)	14
The Lady of Lyons	(Lytton)	14
Richard III	(Shakespeare)	13
Black-Ey'd Susan	(Jerrold)	12
Raby Rattler	Stirling)	12
Cherry & Fair Star	(n.k.)	12

No other piece is recorded more than eight times. (It should, perhaps, be noted that in most contemporary sources only the main presentation of the evening was recorded. It has not, therefore, been possible to assess afterpieces in the same way.)

Even allowing for the incomplete nature of the evidence, twenty-six recorded performances of *Mungo Park* make this play worthy of closer attention. Park was an explorer who died in Africa in 1806. Charles Dibdin produced a play with this title at Sadler's Wells in 1816 and Allardyce Nicoll lists a version of 1840 by B. Bernard. This latter text was printed in *Oxberry's Budget* in 1844 and would have entered the Wild repertoire at that time. The play as it is printed in Oxberry is not particularly interesting, lacking drama and excitement, but rewritten as a vehicle for first 'Nelson' and then other dogs trained by Sam it became a great attraction. The original sub-title of *African Treachery* was changed to *The Sailor and His Dogs*, thereby placing the piece firmly in the category of "nautical/canine" instead of the more general "melodrama of action" as it is described in *Oxberry*. Proof of its drawing power is demonstrated by its frequent choice for benefit nights, Sam selecting it on six occasions and Williams, the black actor who created the role of Snowball, the cabin boy in the piece, on three [2].

Dog dramas were popular everywhere at this time and were not confined to the booth theatres. At Halifax Theatre Royal in 1839, for example, 'Hector' and 'Bruin' were starring in *The Slave's Revenge* and at Wakefield in 1853 the "celebrated dogs" of Messrs. Matthew and Harrison achieved a great success in *The Forest of Bondy*. It is not surprising, therefore, that the "caninized" version of *Mungo Park* and also *The Pirate Ship: or, The Dog of the Wave* should feature regularly on the programme. Nor, indeed, that *Black-Ey'd Susan* and *Raby Rattler* should be recorded with some frequency, since these highly successful melodramas were played everywhere, at major and minor theatres alike. *Cherry and Fair Star* was an adaptable piece of spectacle, advertised at different times as "an interesting drama" and as a pantomime. Around Christmas and Easter it often ran for several performances, not a normal occurrence at that time, and this may partly explain why it has been recorded so often. [3]

To find Lord Lytton's dignified drama, *The Lady of Lyons* in the "top ten" might seem a little unexpected. Mrs. Sam Wild certainly enjoyed playing Pauline (p. 224), but no management could afford to present a piece frequently just because the leading lady liked the title role: there must have been public demand. A closer examination of the data reveals that at least eight of the fourteen recorded performances were special occasions—charity benefits, request or command performances, or during the engagement of a guest star. Such events brought the kind of audience that appreciated Lytton's style.

Ten of Shakespeare's plays were in the Wild repertoire but only four —*Hamlet, Macbeth, Othello* and *Richard III*—are recorded with any frequency. It should be noted that we are not talking here of abbreviated fairground performances where "*Hamlet* and *Othello* were both barbarously murdered for the gratification of the early risers at least five-and-twenty times before breakfast", but of full-length productions. The texts, however, would not have been Shakespeare's originals and would have emphasised the action and excitement while cutting down proportionately on the worlds. *Macbeth*, which was advertised "with the original music of Locke" was probably Charles Dibdin's "melo-dramatisation" of 1819 which in turn was based on Davenant's 1674 adaptation. Davenant built up the witch scenes and introduced a good deal of singing and dancing. To do justice to this musical tragedy, Sam Wild engaged local singers to assist with the choruses [4].

It might be suspected that contemporary observers (and, indeed, Sam Wild himself) would be inclined to emphasise Shakespearean productions and thus bias the data. Close checking, however, reveals no evidence of such a trend. All the indications are, in fact, that the plays of Shakespeare were regarded in very much the same light as the popular dramas of the day and received the same amount of attention both from Sam and from the press. The following report in the *Era* of 6 May 1849 (also quoted in Sam's memoirs), illustrates this:

> On Wednesday and Thursday, *The Flowers of the Forest* . . . the Wolf of Mr. John Holloway and Mrs. S. Wild's Cynthia were beyond all praise. On Friday *Richard III*, Mr. Holloway's Richard was a powerful delineation. On Monday and Tuesday was performed *My Poor Dog Tray: or, The Idiot of the Shannon*. Mr. Bateson as Darby Sullivan was exceedingly droll and played and sung admirably. Mr. S. Wild's celebrated dog, Nelson, surpassed anything of the kind hitherto witnessed on these boards.

Patriotism and spectacle were reliable attractions in the nineteenth-century theatre, and dramatisations of famous battles in which Britain had featured prominently, such as Trafalgar or Waterloo, were naturally in the Wild repertoire. When patriotism and spectacle were combined with the immediate interest of current events, a success was guaranteed, and the evidence suggests that Old Wild's was not slow to take advantage of suitable occasions. Two such topical dramatisations, dealing with the Crimean War and with the Indian Mutiny, are referred to in Sam Wild's reminiscences; a third, not mentioned there, was the Second Sikh War.

This war broke out in India in 1848 and was finally brought under control in mid-1849. In January 1850, during a winter season at Carlisle, Old Wild's brought out *The War in India*, described as both a "new drama" and a "magnificent spectacle". From surviving playbills it is evident that this is a re-working of W. T. Moncrieff's 1823 piece, *The Cataract of the Ganges*. The change of title, however, and the introduction of personalities who had featured in the Sikh rebellion, such as Sir Charles Napier, leave no doubt that Wild's was taking advantage of public interest in recent affairs. [5]

The Crimean War was the first real conflict in which the British had been involved for nearly forty years, and in the early stages public pride and patriotism were very much aroused. Britain declared war on Russia on 27 March 1854, and at Blackburn on 17 April Wild's was presenting "a local drama, based on the late stirring events representing the Russian and Turkish war at the Battle of Kalafat" [*Era*, 23.4.1854]. Dr. J. S. Bratton, in her study of the Crimean War on the London stage, estimates that between 1854 and 1855, at least twenty-five plays dealing with this subject were produced in the capital, the earliest dating from around mid-April 1854 [6]. Wild's *Battle of Kalafat* must have been one of the first provincial dramatisations of a war in which the British had yet to play an active part. Like the first London productions, it did not have a great deal of factual material of which to make use, and to judge from an admittedly patronising report in the *Preston Pilot* of 10 June 1854, was little more than a basic stock drama with a few additions in the way of costumes and extras:

We were just in time to hear the gentleman in yellow leggings that we had seen outside, while gazing steadfastly at the brown canvass top of the tent, call on "yon blue 'even to bring down rewing on their teraytors' 'eds", a prayer that was answered by the clown, harlequin, pantaloon, and gentleman in crimson stockings, and all the ladies of the company rushing in at the sides, when a general conflict took place, and amidst the clashing of swords and the shrieks of the ladies, in marched the grey-coated military at the back of the stage, fired their muskets in the air, and disappeared at the same time as the curtain dropped.

The news of the Battle of the Alma and, a year later, the eventual fall of Sebastopol, provided the theatres with plenty of dramatic material. By the latter date, as Dr. Bratton observes, there was already considerable public disillusionment with the way in which the war had been mismanaged, and this was reflected in some of the later London presentations. This disillusionment, however, does not seem to have percolated down to the booth-going public of the industrial north, and Sam's description of the finale of *The Fall of Sebastopol* conjures up a scene of exuberant patriotism with complete confidence in British might and superiority (pp. 123–4).

The savage events of the Indian Mutiny took place between May and September 1857, and the horrific details of the Cawnpore Massacre aroused great fury in England. Old Wild's dramatisation of the main events of this war (frequently adapted and called, at various times, *The Siege of Delhi*, *The Fall of Delhi*, *The Murder at Cawnpore*, *The Cawnpore Massacre*, *The Sepoy Revolt*, *The Siege of Lucknow*, *The Relief of Lucknow*, etc.), came out at Wigan in January 1858, some two months after the first London production. In addition, *The War in India* was revived and both pieces were played at frequent intervals during that year and in 1859. The company's pièce de résistance, a gigantic model elephant (mistaken by many, according to report, for the real thing), cheerfully did duty for both spectacles, as did Sir Charles Napier who really had no place in the Mutiny drama [7]. An account in the *Preston Guardian* of 29 May 1858 of *The Siege of Delhi* indicates that it, too, was little more than a stock drama with appropriate (and inappropriate) characters hurriedly fitted in:

The plot was not very well described, and we were at a loss to know which was Nana Sahib and which the King of Delhi. Nor could we make out what Charles Napier was doing there, although the gallant general fought with his well-known courage no less than six combats against all kinds of odds. [The play] was brought to a close by a grand combat, all of the male characters taking part. The total absence of malice in the arrangement of this grand duello was truly gratifying, the combatants going through what is known by dancers as the "link and chain", and by this means Sir Charles Napier was enabled to have a friendly "set to" with Sir Colin Campbell, while the King of Delhi nearly "did for" Nana Sahib.

From time to time Wild's presented other topical pieces, unconnected with British military exploits. In 1849, for example, at the height of the gold-rush fever, *California: or, The Land of Gold* was staged, and in 1852 *Bloomers!* satirised the attempt by Mrs. Amelia Bloomer to introduce a more rational costume for women. *The Ocean Monarch: or, The Ship on Fire*, staged at Heywood in 1848, was more serious in content, being a dramatisation of a recent and local catastrophe. The ship of the title, an emigrant boat, caught fire just outside Liverpool in August 1848, and over four hundred lives were lost. Wild's was one of the first companies to stage this drama, penned in haste by C. R. Somerset [8]. A production at the Liver Theatre in Liverpool, a week or two after Wild's presentation, drew a disapproving reaction from the *Theatrical Times* of 18 November 1848:

It is founded, as may be supposed, on the late lamentable occurrence in this part; and whatever may be the excellence of the piece as a dramatic production, which we doubt not, we must assert our disapprobation of making use of such a late accident for such a purpose. Even now there are many of the bereaved sufferers in the towns to whom the very mention of the disaster overwhelms them with grief.

On many occasions, also, Old Wild's managed to acquire new dramas very shortly after their London premieres. A number of highly successful pieces were brought out within a year of their first performance in the capital and some even sooner. *The Green Bushes*, *The Colleen Bawn* and *Lady Audley's Secret*, for example, were all staged at Wild's within twelve months and adaptations of Mrs. Beecher Stowe's slavery novels, *Uncle Tom's Cabin* and *Dred*, were brought out barely one month and three months respectively after the first London versions. The speed with which *Uncle Tom* was produced can be explained by the fact that it was dramatised by a member of the company. With *It is Never Too Late to Mend*, Old Wild's would appear to have stolen a march on the metropolis, since an adaptation of Charles Reade's novel was staged at the booth in October 1858 and there is no record of a London performance before 1860. This is probably not the full picture, however, since there are likely to have been several unlicensed, and therefore unrecorded, versions running before that time. Reade, like Dickens, waged unceasing war against the hack dramatists who pirated his work, but he could do little about provincial representations [9].

Old Wild's ability to present new dramas at short notice was due to Sam's foresight in two matters: the correspondence he kept up with minor dramatists (p. 77) and his subscription to the Dramatic Authors' Society. The latter was an association set up by long-suffering popular playwrights after the Dramatic Copyright Act of 1833, to make some attempt at obtaining royalties from companies who performed their plays. It was not usual for the proprietors of travelling theatres to indulge in such expensive formalities, as J. R. R. Planché, one of the founder members of the Society, makes clear:

> Of course there were freebooters, in this as well as other professions, who had a more lofty disdain for the distinctions of *meum* and *tuum*, and who, not being worth powder and shot, carried on their depredations openly with impunity. These unscrupulous persons were thorns in the side not only of the authors but of respectable managers, under whose very noses they opened portable theatres or booths, in which they played for nothing pieces the others honestly paid for, frequently anticipating their production at the regular theatre and therefore diminishing their attraction. This was a very reasonable cause of complaint to the society from honourable managers with whom we were in regular communication. Unfortunately, however, we had no power to protect them, as these offenders were, like the ghost in *Hamlet*, 'here', 'there' and 'gone' before a writ could be served upon them. [10]

A number of Sam Wild's contemporaries were certainly guilty of this charge. Samuel Pickles, a close acquaintance, even had the honour of being identified by name in Edward Stirling's memoirs as one who had "laid violent hands on my pieces for many years, defying the Act of Parliament and myself" [11].

Twelve pounds per annum was quite a considerable sum to pay for permission to perform particular plays (p. 201), and the fact that Sam Wild was willing to part with this amount when many of his fellow-travellers did not see any reason so to do, is indicative of his very real desire to be considered "respectable"—a theme which is echoed again and again throughout his reminiscences. Having paid his subscription, however, Sam made full use of the fact for the purposes of self-advertisement, announcing it at the head of playbills and displaying placards outside his booth to the same effect. The *Preston Guardian* of 3 June 1857 commended this responsible behaviour:

> We were particularly gratified to learn that Mr. Wild duly respected the claims of literature. He scorned, indeed, to steal the products of an author's brain. If we take his word for it, we may believe that he only produces most legitimate dramas and that he pays most legitimately for the use of the acting copyrights. Does he not indeed expressly say that he has "entered into an especial agreement with the Dramatic Authors' Society to play the whole of their pieces"? We take it for granted a respectable showman never tells a lie, and we implicitly believed Mr. Wild on Monday.

As has already been noted, the audience at Old Wild's frequently had the opportunity of seeing new dramas which had only recently been premiered in London. Sam himself claimed that he never visited the same town twice "without having on the second occasion of my visit, something new wherewith to please my patrons" (p. 198). An analysis has been made of all seasons for which more than seven titles are recorded, to establish the proportion of new to old pieces at different periods in the life of Old Wild's.

The general trend revealed is as follows: up to 1857 or thereabouts, "new" dramas (i.e. those of five years old or less) formed between one-third and one-half of the pieces recorded for each season. From 1858 onwards, however, the proportion of new pieces gets lower, forming about one-sixth of the total in 1863. If the distinction between "new" and "old" is set at ten years instead of five, the trend is the same. A similar result is obtained even if, somewhat optimistically, "new" dramas are taken to be those less than twenty years old. Plays from the previous century, such as *Pizarro*, *The Stranger* and *The Iron Chest* remained in the repertoire up to the last years of Old Wild's; but these pieces were also popular in major theatres until well into the second half of the nineteenth century.

The number of afterpieces recorded is considerably smaller than the number of main dramas, but these too have been analysed. Here the proportion of new to old never exceeds one-third and is down to one-sixth by the mid-1840's, indicating less pressure for novelty in this section of the programme. Overall the evidence suggests that the repertoire of Old Wild's was becoming a little old-fashioned rather before the 1860's, which is the period from which Sam dates the company's decline. It is not surprising, therefore, that Old Wild's found itself unable to compete successfully with the newer attractions of the developing towns.

The typical programme at Old Wild's consisted of a drama and a farce with singing and dancing between the pieces. During the run of a fair, this programme remained in outline the same but was compressed into a very short space of time. Sam remarks that on these occasions they measured their successes "not so much by the quality of the performance given as by the number of them that could be got through in a day" (p. 61). Contemporary sources bear this out: one fairgoer noted of Wild's: "Here plays were gone through with great consideration for the patience of the auditory, not lasting longer than twenty minutes each" [12]. Another, disappointed, patron commented:

> Within a quarter of an hour's time of our first ascending the steps of the show, we found ourselves descending them again, confirmed in our opinion that shows now are not the shows they used to be. [*Preston Pilot* 10.6.1854]

A certain skill was needed in cutting plays to fairtime length so that as much display and action as possible was left in while time-consuming dialogue was omitted. Peter Paterson recorded how *The Castle Spectre*, which in a major theatre would have taken nearly three hours, could in a booth be completed in about twelve minutes [13], and a clown interviewed by Henry Mayhew summarised the procedure:

> We used to knock *Robert the Devil* into a very little space, doing the

scenes but cutting them short; and as for the pantomime, we had scarcely commenced with "Two more slaves will I rise out of the unfathomable deep" than we were singing, "Our pantomime's done, here's an end to our fun". Sometimes the people would grumble awful, and at others they laughed to see how they was swindled. [14]

The emphasis for these fairtime programmes, then, was on noise, colour and music rather than on dramatic achievement, and indeed the limits imposed on the length of the pieces allowed little time for gradual unfolding of plot or action. This frequently left the audience confused as to what exactly was going on: as, for example, at Preston in 1857 where Old Wild's was presenting the ten-minute version of *The Dogs of the Plantation: or, A British Sailor in his Glory*:

We could not, at all events, fathom its depth or follow its scheme of cause and consequence ... The situations were striking and the dialogue ... incomprehensible; but then the fencing—and there were six combats—told for itself; and the performance of the celebrated dogs, Nelson and Lion, required no explanation. [*Preston Guardian* 3.6.1857]

Military spectacles were ideal for fairground performances, affording plenty of scope for noise and display—as at Leeds Fair in 1854 where three rival booth theatres all used the Crimean War to attract an audience:

The "legitimate drama" was provided by Mr. Pickuls [*sic*], Mr. Wild and Mr. Templeton, who presented and represented the Turco–Russian war with all its details and with every variety of graphic and thrilling effect, from the passage of Pruth to the bombardment of Odessa and the siege of Silistria. Mr. Wild claimed the van with a formidable array of Russian and Turkish soldiers, armed *cap-à-pie*, and a gorgeous display of barmerets [*sic*] of all nations; but the claim was disputed by Mr. Pickuls who clothed his dramatis personae in glittering coats of mail and astonished the crowd with the brilliant *pas* of his *danseuse*. Mr. Templeton brought up the rear with a meagre display . . . in which the war with Russia was commenced and concluded in the short space of five minutes. [*Leeds Mercury* 15.7.1854]

Outside fairtime the programme expanded into a full evening's entertainment with a main drama and a farce or pantomime of normal length, together with a couple of songs or dances between the pieces. This standard format could change on special occasions such as the benefit night of one of the performers. At these times the pieces chosen were generally those in which the beneficiary appeared to best advantage, and two full-length dramas might be played instead of one drama and a farce. When Sam Wild took his benefit he always chose pieces in which he could shine as a nautical hero and where, if possible, the dogs could appear as an added attraction. At Bradford in 1844 he chose *Gallant Paul* and *The Red Indian and his Dog*; at Preston in 1850 it was *Mungo Park*; and at Dewsbury in 1858, *The Ferryman and his Dogs* and *Black-Ey'd Susan* [15]. His son Tom, on the other hand, developed as he grew up a talent for both clowning and stage fights and chose accordingly for his benefit at Wakefield in 1861:

> *Jessy Vere* and *The Mountain Pirate* were the pieces, in which there was abundant scope for the exercise of his talents as Low Comedian. His broadsword combat with Mr. Wood was remarkably clever. [*Era* 11.11.1861].

Patronage nights were also occasions for special programmes when the pieces were usually chosen by the "distinguished guests". Shakespeare and the quality dramatists of the day were often selected, *Hamlet* and *The Lady of Lyons* being especial favourites, but this was not inevitably the case. The Marquis of Douro's party, probably the most genuinely distinguished guests ever to visit Old Wild's, opted for *Mungo Park* and *Every Inch a Sailor* in order to see more of 'Nelson' the wonder dog [16].

Now and again two full-length dramas were presented on one programme as an added attraction on what would otherwise have been an ordinary evening. In all recorded instances of this happening at Wild's (seven in all), it was at the end of a particularly long stay in a town and presumably acted as an inducement to the local population for whom by that time the novelty of theatregoing might have worn off.

Very little evidence has been found of particular dramas or types of drama finding more favour at one town than at another. Michael Booth has suggested that the success of nautical melodrama at London's Surrey Theatre was due at least in part to the large proportion of sailors and quayside workers in the audience [17]. It might therefore be supposed that nautical pieces would be recorded more frequently for Wild's seasons at Hull or Preston than for inland towns like Bradford or Huddersfield. This was not found to be the case, however, such dramas being recorded with the same frequency throughout the towns on the circuit. Overall, indeed, no one type of melodrama predominates in any one area. The "legitimate" drama, too, although forming only a small part of the repertoire, is fairly well distributed, *The Lady of Lyons* in particular being recorded for almost every town on the circuit.

There are a few instances of dramas with a local interest being presented. J. S. Coyne's *Did You Ever Send Your Wife to Camberwell?* was presented at Hull with the substitution of Beverley for Camberwell and at Carlisle with Gretna Green. Both *The Oldham Recruit* and *The Bradford Cobbler* were staged at Bradford. These were all farces: there is no record of a main drama with local interest, apart from *The Ocean Monarch* referred to earlier in this chapter. There was also a winter season at Huddersfield in 1863 when out of fifteen main dramas recorded, four were Irish in subject—a type previously almost unknown in the Wild repertoire. Three different guest stars chose to star in pieces with an Irish hero, and in one case an earlier drama, *The Wild Flower of Mexico* was adapted to become *The Wild Flower of Erin*. This almost certainly coincided with an influx of Irish immigrant workers to the factories of the district [18].

When comparing the plays presented in summer and in winter seasons, it is necessary to keep in mind that winter seasons at Wild's were, as a rule, better reported in the press. This was probably because the local newspapers were used more for advertising during the longer winter seasons and responded by taking more notice of the theatre. There is, therefore, a greater body of information available for the winter months than for the rest of the year.

Even with this proviso in mind one major difference, already touched on briefly in Chapter 3, may be noted. This concerns the presentation of the works of Shakespeare and the major nineteenth-century dramatists such as Bulwer-Lytton and Sheridan Knowles. These were largely confined to the winter months when guest stars were engaged. This gives rise to two questions: 1) why should the performance of Shakespeare and other major dramatists be confined to the periods when guest stars were appearing?; and 2) why should guest stars only be engaged during winter seasons?

The answer to the first lies with Sam Wild himself. In the early years, while his parents still managed the company, one actor was usually engaged to play the leading tragic roles each season. One or more of the Holloway brothers filled this position for many years [19]. Sam, however, took great pride in his own acting ability and his delight in starring roles is evident from his recollections. He tells us, nevertheless, that he did not play the major Shakespearean characters and "never aspired much to tragedy" (p. 21). It is understandable, therefore, that on taking over the management he should choose those dramas in which he himself could play leading roles. In so doing, he not only kept himself in the limelight but also saved the salary of another leading man.

With regard to the second question, it is likely that guest stars were not engaged during summer seasons because there was no need for them. The stay in each town was comparatively short, and the company normally moved on before it outstayed its welcome. During the winter, on the other hand, it was customary, indeed necessary, to remain in one town for four or five months. Appendix (C) gives details of all guest stars known to have appeared at Old Wild's; from this it will be seen that they were generally engaged from January onwards when the company had already been in situ for the same period as the longest booth season. The guest stars, therefore, would have been engaged for the purpose of reviving falling attendance figures and also, perhaps, to attract those who were not in the habit of attending the theatre regularly. This theory is given weight by Sam's statement that at Keighley during the 1859–60 season he engaged no stars "as things were so flourishing we had no need of them" (p. 187).

Although some of the earlier guest stars (Arthur Nelson the clown, for example, and Juba the black dancer) belonged rather more to the world of popular entertainment, the later years show a succession of guest actors with almost entirely classical repertoires. Contemporary references in the *Era* and other journals show that these actors were known for their renderings of the major tragic roles. It follows, therefore, that they were engaged by Wild's specifically for their personal repertoire. This argues that although Sam knew he could, under normal circumstances, attract an audience by presenting a succession of melodramas and spectacles, there was also a demand for the "legitimate" drama in the towns he visited. Otherwise, he would certainly not have been willing to step down from the leading role and pay the fees demanded by guest stars.

Another, though less marked, difference between summer and winter seasons is in consecutive performances of specific pieces. During summer seasons a drama was only repeated if the demand was particularly strong. At Hull in 1844, for example, *Isabelle*, presented for the first time on 21 October, was repeated the following night, "in consequence of overflowing houses and immense success". Similarly, *The Jewess*, staged on 28 October, was repeated three days later "on account of the great number of Ladies and Gentlemen who were not able to gain admission to the Theatre on Monday last" [20].

During winter seasons consecutive performances were more common, a new piece often being advertised in advance for a two-day run. This was normally on a Monday and Tuesday, giving the management the option, if the new drama were a success, of repeating it towards the end of the week. Longer runs were unusual and only occurred when the play was an exceptional attraction as, for example, Wild's speedy dramatisation of *Uncle Tom's Cabin* or the topical and highly patriotic *Battle of the Alma* (p. 117). The normal practice was to revive a successful piece one or more times during the season, as was the case with *It Is Never Too Late To Mend*, which was repeated four times at Burnley between November 1858 and February 1859 [21].

Although dramas were frequently announced on the playbills as being "in preparation", the actual advance planning of the programme in both summer and winter was kept as flexible as possible to allow for unexpected successes or failures, public demand or change in circumstances. The company had to be adaptable and ready to play any one of a large number of pieces at very short notice. This was part of life in every booth theatre: Mark Melford, in his autobiography, recalls his first engagement:

"Well", continued the proprietress, "you can join tonight. We find all the wardrobe—no end of shirts, tights and square cuts—and you can go on as 'Oratio in Hamlet—sing two songs in between and play Nipper in the farce." "That will do to start with", said I, "and the songs are ready if the band can vamp me on and off; and as for the farce", I said, "what is it?" "Oh! we never bothers about that until the curtain's down on the drama ..." [22]

Research indicates that overall the bigger travelling theatres had much the same repertoire and frequently set up in direct opposition to one another: Old Wild's anticipated Parrish's production of *Jack Sheppard* at Bradford (pp. 56–58), and Edwards managed to stage *Belphegor* before Wild's could do so (p. 97). Few booth companies took as much trouble as did Wild's to keep *The Era* and other journals informed of their affairs, and as a result information on their repertoires is limited. A collection of playbills for Thorne's booth during a summer season at North Shields in 1845, however, yields some useful information.

Over half the pieces presented by Thorne's during that season are also in Wild's repertoire, and the blend of melodrama, spectacle, pantomime and farce is much the same. At Thorne's, however, Shakespeare was presented regularly during the summer season with no suggestion of guest actors or special occasions, which points to a different policy within that company's management with regard to starring roles. Mr. Thorne himself rarely took part in productions (his only appearance that season was in a farce) and it is likely that the company possessed a strong leading tragedian who could play the Shakespearean parts.

The poorer travelling theatres, with less resources to spare for the purchasing of new plays, tended to present rather shoddier fare than the bigger booths—such as one which was observed at Preston in 1859:

> Near to Wild's was a smaller, shabby concern, in which the performances were of a strange medley kind, including, according to a notice suspended in front of the show: "War in the East—songs —lovers' quarrels—one penny". [*Preston Pilot* 18.6.1859]

Sam's brother, Tom, seems to have descended into this category after the division of the family business in 1856, since we find *The Era* of 3 January 1858 administering a reproof for the "slight and flimsy pieces" offered by his company:

> Dewsbury requires something more legitimate than such pieces as 'Far Far at Sea', 'Broken Sword', 'Cottager's Daughter', etc. The comic pantomime seems the only attraction offered to the public.

When one looks at the towns visited regularly by Old Wild's, it is surprising how many of them already possessed an established theatre.

Blackburn, Bradford, Halifax, Hull, Leeds, Preston and Wakefield were all on the circuit yet all had their own permanent theatres. These were not, of course, open all the year round, the manager of any particular theatre circuit moving his company from one to another and opening each for a season. They did, however, usually open for the fair week, and were thus normally in direct opposition to Old Wild's and other booth theatres. The programme for one week at three different Theatres Royal on the Wild circuit are set out below: [23]

Leeds, 1845	Hull, 1850	Preston, 1863
Eugene Aram	Othello	Catherine Howard
The Lost Ship	Father & Daughter	The Factory Girl
Black-Ey'd Susan	Dumb Man of M'Cr.	The Black Doctor
Poll & Partner Joe	Two Galley Slaves	Belphegor
The Stranger	The Wild Boy	Il Trovatore
Don Caesar de Bazan	Foundling of the Forest	Dark Deeds
The Green Bushes	Inkeeper of Abbeville	The Lady of Lyons

There is a marked similarity here, not only to the specific plays in Wild's repertoire but also to the general type of plays presented. Where one might expect the major disparity to lie would be in the actual presentation and staging of the plays; and this is the subject of the final chapter.

REFERENCES

1. Playbill collections, Bradford and Hull Central Libraries.
2. Arundell, D. *The Story of Sadler's Wells*, 1965, 97; *Oxberry's Budget*, 26.2.1844. Information obtained from the *Era*.
3. Playbill collections, Bankfield Museum Halifax and Wakefield Central Library.
4. *Preston Guardian*, 2.6.1855; O. W. 142; Arundell, D., *op. cit.* 96; Odell, G. C. D., *Shakespeare from Betterton to Irving*, first pub. 1920, this ed. 1963, 28–29.
5. *Era*, 27.1.1850 & 23.4.1850.
6. Bratton, J. S., "Theatre of war: the Crimea on the London stage 1854–5" *in* Bradby D., James L. and Sharratt B. (eds), *Performance and Politics in Popular Drama* 1980, 120.
7. O. W., 161; *Preston Herald*, 29.5.1858.
8. *Era*, 17.6.1849; *ibid* 16.5.1852; *Theatrical Times*, 11.11.1848.
9. Playbill collection Hull Central Library; also O. W. 209; *Era*, 7.11.1852, 8.2.1857 & 31.10.1858; Coryton, J., *Stageright*, 1873.
10. Planche, J. R. R., *Recollections and Reflections*, 1901, 39.
11. Stirling, E., *Old Drury Lane*, 1881, 176.
12. *Preston Pilot*, 18.6.1859.

13.   "Peter Paterson", pseud. of Bertram, J. G., *Glimpses of Real Life*, 1864, 94–106.
14.   Mayhew, H., *op. cit.*, Vol. III, 128.
15.   O. W., 66; *Era* 16.6.1850 & 22.8.1858.
16.   O. W., 83.
17.   Booth, M., *English Melodrama*, 1965, 102.
18.   Playbill collections, Bradford and Hull Central Libraries; *Era*, 20.1.1850 & 15.3.1863; *Oxberry's Budget*, 26.2.1844.
19.   O. W., 86; also numerous playbills & newspaper reports.
20.   Playbill collection, Hull Central Library.
21.   *Era*, 5.12.1858 & 30.1.1859.
22.   Melford, M., *My Life in a Booth and Something More*, 1913, 18.
23.   *Leeds Times*, 8.11.1845; playbill collection Hull Central Library; *Preston Pilot*, 23.5.1863.

CHAPTER 5

THE STAGING OF PLAYS AT OLD WILD'S

The period spanned by Sam Wild's memoirs was one of increasing extravagance in theatrical presentation. As George Rowell says:

> The staple fare of the early Victorian theatre was spectacle, and spectacle, whether in the form of melodrama, opera, ballet, extravaganza, pantomime or Shakespearean pageant, demanded a far more elaborate style of staging than the Georgian theatre had afforded. (1)

A study of Wild's repertoire reveals that many of the main pieces depended for their success upon special scenic or mechanical effects. Most of these dramas had originally been written for large London theatres which possessed all the necessary facilities such as scene-painting rooms, flying and backstage space, and all the latest complex stage machinery. It is therefore of considerable interest to see how such dramas were interpreted within the confines of a booth theatre. This chapter examines the staging of plays at Old Wild's, both with regard to the overall approach of the management to the presentation of pieces and with reference to specific technical details.

It has already been seen in Chapter 1 that in terms of size and facilities there was little difference between the portable booth and the semi-permanent winter theatre. It has not been thought necessary, therefore, to treat these two locations separately in the present context, although where relevant the type of building has been noted.

Booth theatres have not hitherto been considered as serious alternatives to the more permanent homes of the drama. Writers like Pierce Egan, Peter Paterson and Charles Dickens set the tone which has prevailed down to the present day: one of amused, patronising observation of a quaint form of entertainment which could in no way be compared with "real" theatre. Michael Booth sums up the accepted view of performances in the portable booths:

Other stages as well as those in theatres presented melodrama. Booth theatres gave drastically shortened versions of well-known melodramas; even Shakespearean tragedies were jammed into half an hour, with everything cut out but ghosts, murders, combats and thrills; dialogue was improvised by the actors. [2]

It is certainly true, as already noted in previous chapters, that during fairtime truncated versions of popular pieces were presented. It has not been sufficiently recognised, however, that these fair-day performances represented only a part of the travelling theatre's business. A company like Wild's would arrive in town several days before the fair and could stay on, if permission were granted, for several weeks afterwards. During the actual fair-days the short programme would be repeated as often as the booth could be filled; outside the fair-days, plays were performed in their entirety. During winter seasons, too, usually lasting from November to March, full-length programmes were presented every evening. In a company such as Wild's, therefore, a greater proportion of the year was spent in presenting dramas in their original length than in putting on abbreviated versions; and it is the former with which we are now concerned.

"So far as the limitations of our establishment would allow", says Sam Wild, ". . . we always endeavoured to do justice to all the plays we produced" (p. 142). While this is the kind of statement any theatrical manager might be expected to make, the evidence indicates that in fact a good deal of attention was paid to the presentation of pieces, with regard both to preparation and to "dressing"—i.e. scenery and costume.

Michael Booth states that in the portable theatres dialogue was improvised by the actors and indeed in some of the smaller booths this does seem to have been the case. The clown interviewed by Henry Mayhew stated categorically, "You see, the performances consisted of all gag. I don't suppose anyone knows what the words are in the piece"; and one of the requirements of the company joined by Mark Melford was that he should be able to improvise at length. Another of Mayhew's interviewees, however, differentiated between the smaller and the larger booths in this respect:

When old Richardson was alive, he used to make actors study their parts regularly; and there's Thorne's and Bennett's and Douglas's and other large travelling concerns that do so at the present time; but where there's one that does, there's ten that don't. [3]

Wild's was certainly one of the shows that did insist upon preparation: there are several textual references to daily rehearsals, and it is significant that one occasion upon which John Holloway found himself obliged to "gag" (when Old Wild's was endeavouring to present *Jack Sheppard* before a rival) is remembered by Sam as an incident out of the ordinary. [4]

Many of the surviving playbills acknowledge either a producer or a stage manager. Up to about 1844 a succession of people seem to have held this position, but from that time onwards Sam's name is the only one which appears. Direction in the sense we understand it today was not yet part of theatrical production, the stage manager effectively controlling the preparation and presentation of a new drama. The acknowledgement of a producer or stage manager by name on the bills is evidence of the importance assigned to this role at Old Wild's. Mark Melford's recollections (quoted in the previous chapter) show that by no means all travelling theatres regarded the finer points of production as important; and Barry Jackson found much the same situation obtaining in the very last days of the portables, during the Second World War:

> Pressure of time prevented serious study and I gathered that only one complete text was assimilated—*East Lynne*. This, with some tags from the Bible and Shakespeare, served all productions. The actors were told the outline of the plot and were then thrown on to the stage to fill out the dialogue to the best of their ability. [5]

An extensive and varied wardrobe was essential for any theatrical company wishing to succeed and this seems to have been recognised at Old Wild's from an early date. Such incidents as the hiring out of dresses for a masked ball, the purchasing of the court dresses of Louis Philippe and the retention of a permanent wardrobe mistress all point to a reasonable standard in custome. Even when poverty had forced disbandment of the company in the late 1860's, the wardrobe was still considered attractive enough to be hired for a season by two major theatres [6].

Similarly a large and varied stock of scenery was considered a necessity at any well-run theatre. Sam's reminiscences make frequent reference to fresh scenery being painted for each new production, and some weight is given to these assertions by the actual identification of the various scenic artists by name: Wallett, for example, who joined the company in that capacity in the 1830s before he came a famous clown; Liver, who held the post in the 1840s when old Mrs. Wild was in charge; Hope, who combined the job with that of band-leader in the 1850s; and several others [7]. Surviving playbills corroborate the textual evidence, great emphasis being laid on the company's resources. "Splendid Wardrobe, New and Beautiful Scenery" and "New and Splendid Scenery, Magnificent Dresses" are the claims most frequently made [8], and the same policy was observed in newspaper advertisements, as, for example, that for *The Rajah's Daughter*:

> ... which has been upwards of a fortnight in preparation and brought forward at considerable expense, with all its original splendour, music, marches, processions, and gorgeous appearance. New Scenery. Dresses by Mrs. Meaney. Properties, Extensive Platforms, Palanquins, Etc. by Mr. P. Thomas and Assistants.
> [*Huddersfield Chronicle* 14.12.1850]

Such claims were, of course, accepted practice in nineteenth-century theatrical advertising and should not necessarily be accepted without reservation. One critic noted wryly of Covent Garden that although fresh scenery was advertised for almost every new production, "he must have keen eyes who can discover ... above two scenes out of the twenty that have not slept in the scene-room or become familiar to the sight for several years past"; and the cheapjack William Green, observing the same habit prevailing among fairground shows, suggested that the latter had copied the major theatres:

> One of these travelling mummers is just telling the people free, gratis and for nothing that the scenery and dresses of the entertainment that can be witnessed within cost the management £450! Well done 'old rags and sticks'. I expect you have only multiplied the cost by 200, and then you meant shillings! [9]

Contemporary evidence, however, does bear out Sam Wild's assertions. An old Blackburn resident, recalling the glories of the company's

(Drypool, Augt 1824)

Scott's Theatre.

A CHANGE OF PERFORMANCES EACH DAY
DURING THE FAIR.

Mr. S. begs leave most respectfully to inform the Inhabitants of this Place and the Public in general, that he has fitted up at considerable expence a commodious portable

THEATRE,

Which for neatness of style cannot be surpassed, where he intends bringing forth a succession of NOVELTY during his stay that he trusts will ensure him that Patronage and Support which it will ever be his greatest pride to acknowledge.

THIS DAY

Will be Performed an entire New Grand Melo-Drame, in Two Acts, called

FALSE
Accusation;
OR,
The Knight of the Black Plume.

Prince of Sicily........... Mr M'KENZIE
Ferdinand (aspiring to the throne)....Mr DIRK——Father Uberto (confessor to the Prince)....Mr LISTER
Sicardo... Mr. HADAWAY——Sanguine (his confidant).. Mr. GODDARD
Servants, Officers, &c. by the Company
Florian (Knight of the Black Plume) ....Mr SHEENE——Endora (Wife to Florian).....Mrs WYATT
Ladies, Attendants, &c. by Mesdames RIDDLE, WATSON, &c.

COMIC SONG, " *The good old days of Adam and Eve,*" MR. HADAWAY

The whole to conclude with

An Entire New Pantomime,
CALLED THE

FAIRY
OF THE MOUNTAIN;
Or, Harlequin Runaway.

Fairy of the Mountain....Mrs RUDD——Harlequin.... Mr WATSON——Clown.... Mr. FLOWER
Pantaloon.......... Mr GODDARD——Columbine.......... Mr SHEENE——Constable....... Mr CLARKE
Monsieur Nongtongpaw....Mr HUME—Tinker Mr LIGHTFOOT.. Tailor....Mr JONES

SUCCESSION OF THE SCENES.

1—A Village, and the outside of a Farm House—Tom making love to Patty, but is discovered by her Father—Tom driven from her house, is reduced to a fit of despair, when he is surprised at the appearance of Orpheus, who bequeaths a charm to his pipe, with the power of Magic, which befriends him only to lead others into scrapes, and himself into trouble ; but by the aid of Orpheus, when the transformation takes place—then, slip, slap and away they go, with lots of fun at Scott's Comical Shop.

2—Front view of some place, but nobody knows where ; with a awkward tumble and roll the Butt.

3—Goldbeater's house—an unlucky hit, or the pursuers beat down with the SPRING Arm.

4—Street—Clown turns Portrait Painter, assisted with the power of magic, to create a laugh.

5—Outside of Pastry-Cook's—the Pursuers the wrong side of the door—how to get in is difficult—the art of Knavery prevails—who's there—nobody but us.

6—Inside of ditto, lots of Fruit—make up your mouth—disappointment again—to read the news is difficult—getting into quod easier than getting out of it.

7—Outside of the same—dreadful disasters—gets clear off—with the exception of a shocking disaster—relieving the poor with something hot.

8—Outside of Primrose's Cottage—Sly rogue, got her at last.

9—Interior of ditto—returned home—the escape—two pair of heels better than two pair of heads—frightened to death.

10—Nail him—must go—got the wrong pig by the ear—tip, or go to quod—the Complexion do'nt agree—biter bit, or pocket the affront.

11—More fun—who's the thief—exchange of colours by the Baker and Chimney-sweep.

12—Now for it—a hard run for the fugitives—never too old to learn right—gone again—what's to be done—off again—there they go.

13—Concluding with a New

ENCHANTED CAVERN,
With a finale Dance and Chorus by the whole of the Company.

Boxes, 2s.——Pit, 1s.——Gallery, 6d.

T. TOPPING, PRINTER, 51 LOWGATE, HULL.

Plate 9. The earliest bill yet traced for a north country portable: Scott's Theatre at the Fair at Drypool near Hull, in August 1824. This and Plates 11 and 12 are reproduced by courtesy of the Reference Library, Hull.

Plate 10. William F. Wallett, "The Queen's Jester" (1807–92), a noted circus clown who started his career as scene painter and minor actor with Wild's in the 1830s.

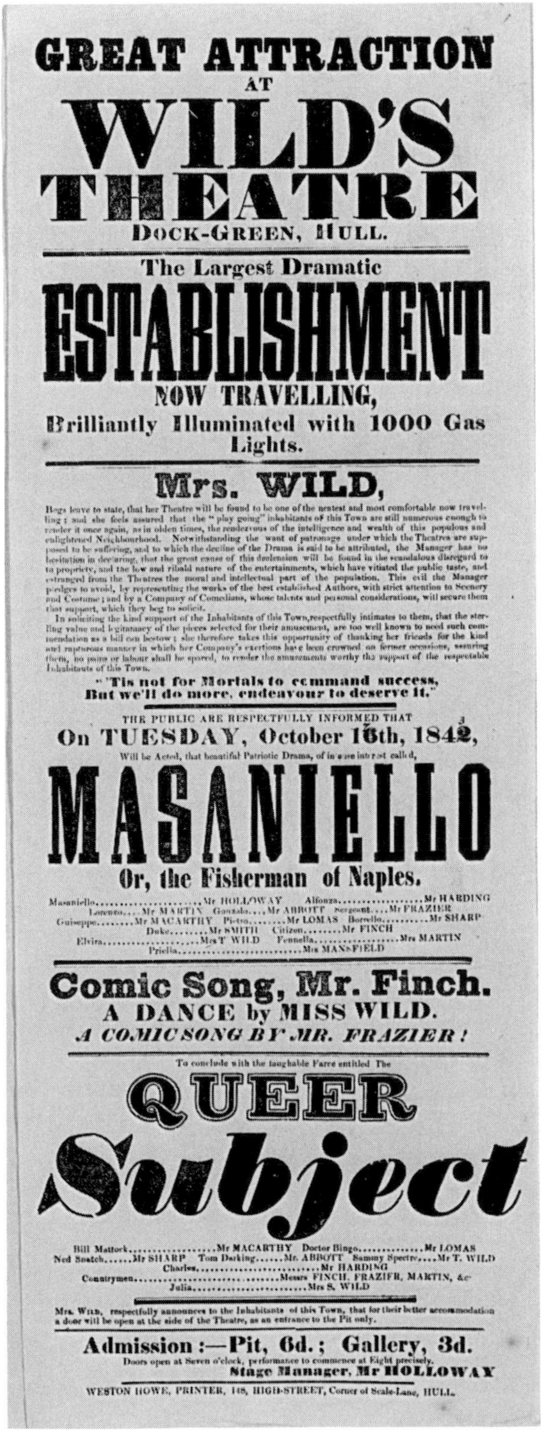

GREAT ATTRACTION
AT
WILD'S
THEATRE
DOCK-GREEN, HULL.

The Largest Dramatic
ESTABLISHMENT
NOW TRAVELLING,
Brilliantly Illuminated with 1000 Gas Lights.

Mrs. WILD,

Begs leave to state, that her Theatre will be found to be one of the neatest and most comfortable now travelling; and she feels assured that the "play going" inhabitants of this Town are still numerous enough to render it once again, as in olden times, the rendezvous of the intelligence and wealth of this populous and enlightened Neighbourhood. Notwithstanding the want of patronage under which the Theatres are supposed to be suffering, and to which the decline of the Drama is said to be attributed, the Manager has no hesitation in declaring, that the great cause of this declension will be found in the scandalous disregard to propriety, and the low and ribald nature of the entertainments, which have vitiated the public taste, and estranged from the Theatres the moral and intellectual part of the population. This evil the Manager pledges to avoid, by representing the works of the best established Authors, with strict attention to Scenery and Costume; and by a Company of Comedians, whose talents and personal considerations, will secure them that support, which they beg to solicit.

In soliciting the kind support of the Inhabitants of this Town, respectfully intimates to them, that the sterling value and legitimacy of the pieces selected for their amusement, are too well known to need such commendation as a bill can bestow; she therefore takes this opportunity of thanking her friends for the kind and rapturous manner in which her Company's exertions have been crowned on former occasions, assuring them, no pains or labour shall be spared, to render the amusements worthy the support of the respectable Inhabitants of this Town.

"'Tis not for Mortals to command success,
But we'll do more, endeavour to deserve it."

THE PUBLIC ARE RESPECTFULLY INFORMED THAT
On TUESDAY, October 16th, 1842,
Will be Acted, that beautiful Patriotic Drama, of in[illegible] interest called,

MASANIELLO
Or, the Fisherman of Naples.

Masaniello........Mr HOLLOWAY Alfonza........Mr HARDING
Lorenzo....Mr MARTIN Gonzalo....Mr ABBOTT Sergeant....Mr FRAZIER
Guiseppe........Mr MACARTHY Pietro........Mr LOMAS Borrello........Mr SHARP
Duke........Mr SMITH Citizen........Mr FINCH
Elvira........Mrs T WILD Fennella........Mrs MARTIN
Priella........Mrs MANSFIELD

Comic Song, Mr. Finch.
A DANCE by MISS WILD.
A COMIC SONG BY MR. FRAZIER!

To conclude with the laughable Farce entitled The

QUEER
Subject

Bill Mattock........Mr MACARTHY Doctor Bingo........Mr LOMAS
Ned Snatch......Mr SHARP Tom Darking......Mr. ABBOTT Sammy Spectre....Mr T. WILD
Charles........Mr HARDING
Countrymen........Messrs FINCH, FRAZIER, MARTIN, &c
Julia........Mrs S. WILD

Mrs. Wild, respectfully announces to the Inhabitants of this Town, that for their better accommodation a door will be open at the side of the Theatre, as an entrance to the Pit only.

Admission :—Pit, 6d.; Gallery, 3d.
Doors open at Seven o'clock, performance to commence at Eight precisely.
Stage Manager, Mr HOLLOWAY

WESTON HOWE, PRINTER, 148, HIGH-STREET, Corner of Scale-Lane, HULL.

Plate 11. "1000 Gas Lights" illuminate the performance of *Masaniello* at Hull in October 1843. Mrs. Wild promises to represent "the works of the best established Authors, with strict attention to Scenery and Costume," and (presumably in lieu of Boxes) offers "a door . . . open at the side of the Theatre, as an entrance to the Pit only."

WILD'S PICTURE GALLERY,
Wellington-Street, Hull.

HOLLO! LOOK HERE!

Second Night of the favourite Drama of Green Bushes!

Mrs. Wild in Order to meet the wishes of her Patrons and Friends, announces that the above admired Drama will be repeated this Evening at Half-price.

Boxes, 1s. ; Pit, 6d. ; Gallery, 3d.

This Evening Friday, Oct 31st, 1845,

Will be presented an entirely new and original Drama, in three acts, produced under the direction of **Mr S. WILD**, entitled

GREEN BUSHES
OR, 100 YEARS AGO.

Connor O'Kennedy - - Mr GRAINGER	George, his younger brother -	Mr BELLAIR
Murtoch. horse jobber, piper, and general Dealer	- -	**Mr. HOLLOWAY**
Paddy Kelly - Mr LOMAS	Larry	Mr FITZGERALD
Ned Keogh, Darby Donoman, Tim O'Toole, (Irish Boys)		Messrs. Lishman, Jones and Howardson
Tom Williams - Mr HUTCHINSON	Servant to George -	Mr JONES
Muster Grinnage, proprietor of a Travelling Caravan - Mr FINCH	Jack Gong, his Man	- Mr S. WILD
Captain Dartoise - Mr JOHNSON	Dennis a Blacksmith -	Mr M·Intyre
GERALDINE, wife to O'Connor		**Mrs MANSFIELD**
Nelly O'Neil -	- Mrs S. WILD	
Miami, the Huntriss of Mississippi		**Mrs MARTIN**
Tigertail, a Squaw - Mrs HOLLOWAY	Eveleen, a child -	Miss S. WILD

A Dance by Miss T WILD

The OLYMPIANS will go through their admired Performances

During which, Mr. HUTCHINSON and his Pupil, Master T. Wild, a child only five years old, will go through a variety of Tricks.

Duet. " Unlucky Pair" Messrs Bellair and Finch

To conclude with the Laughable Farce of The

RAILWAY STATION.

Mr William Smith	Mr Johnson Mr Charles Smith	-	Mr Lomas
Sampson Jones, jun.	- Mr Bellair Mr John Robbins	- Mr Grainger	
Mr Grabbing	- Mr Finch Mr Tap - Mr Lishman Mr Sleeper - Mr Hutchinson Shutup	- Mr Jones	
	Mrs Charles Smith - Mrs Finch Mrs William Smith - Mrs Lomas		

Boxes, 1s.; Pit, 6d. ; Gallery, 3d.

Artist - Mr Fitzgerald   Leader of the Orchestra, Mr Taylor.   Stage Manager, - Mr. S. Wild

Weston Tuxford Howe, Printer, 148, High-Street, Hull.

Plate 12. The second night of *Green Bushes* at Hull—with the first-night raised prices reduced to the standard 1s., 6d. and 3d.

wardrobe, remembered that "young men who wanted a rig-out for pace-egging often appealed to Sam or Tom Wild for assistance". William Green admitted, albeit grudgingly, that Wild's actors were all "gorgeously dressed, kings and queens in any number"; while the unnamed actress who travelled with the show in the 1850's recorded: "the scenery was plentiful and various, the wardrobe extensive and flashy; and there was no lack of thrones, statues, tombs, rocks, balconies or pasteboard banquets" [10]. A report in the *Accrington Free Press* of 16 April 1859, which by its restraint is probably genuine and not written by a member of the company, commented:

> The large booth is fit up in the usual style of travelling theatres, but the stage, dresses, etc. are quite superior to most of them.

Certainly standards among other portables were not always so high. "Cheap" and "frouzy-looking" are the usual epithets applied in contemporary sources, and a report in the *Preston Pilot* of 17 May 1856 confirms, by comparison, Wild's status in the travelling world:

> Close to Wild's was another show of the same description but of a lower grade, which we thought had come from a land where there was a drought upon the earth, at least we imagined so from the fact that to all appearances water had been scarce among the inmates for some days and dirt and faded finery were among the most noticeable marks of the establishment.

When we come to look at specific details of staging in the booth, the first and most important point to make is that in terms of actual performing area Old Wild's differed very little from many major theatres. As was noted in Chapter 1, the stage was normally about 45 feet in working width and about 30 feet in depth. This may be compared with 34 feet in width at Sadler's Wells and 39 feet at the New Standard in Shoreditch where many spectacular pieces were performed. The stage in Richardson's booth, as already mentioned in Chapter 1, was some thirty feet in width.

When discussing Wild's booth, therefore, and those of other large travelling companies such as Thorne's or Parrish's, it is necessary to disabuse our minds of the notion that performances took place in a confined or restricted area. The larger portables had as much onstage space as many a more solidly-built theatre. More space, indeed, in some cases, if we recall Sam's comments on one Theatre Royal occupied by his company for a short period:

> We played our war piece at Wakefield, but the stage being exceedingly small, we were very much restricted in our operations (p. 124).

The war piece in question was *The Siege of Sebastopol* which had received its premiere in the booth at Halifax a month before—obviously in more spacious surroundings.

Richard Southern is of the opinion that the "pair of flats" or sliding scenes which joined together at the back of the stage were in general use until Irving introduced the hanging cloth or drop scene. Research, however, indicates that booth theatres almost invariably used hanging cloths, and indeed the exigencies of travel would make this the only practical technique. At Wild's there was an early morning call on the day of a fair for the men "who had to hang the scenes", and in Star's booth the scenery was described as the kind that "all rolled up". Barry Jackson confirms that drop cloths were still in use in North Wales in the early 1900s, and an actor called Sutton who travelled with an Irish portable in the 1890s gives some useful details:

> Scenery is mounted top and bottom on wooden battens; and there are some managers who fit these with cords and pulleys so that they can be hung in position when the frame is pitched and hauled up or down as required; a cheaper method is to paint a second scene on the back of each cloth, but the other way up, and to change scenes by slinging the floor-batten up to the top of the frame and vice-versa. [11]

Of some 50 surviving Wild playbills, 20 give details of scenery. The number of scenes per drama varies between seven and thirteen, with a total of 180 scenes listed overall. This gives an average of nine scene changes per play, a high number for a booth since the actor with Star's company calculated that about four scenes were normally in use at any one time.

It is likely, of course, that the same scene did duty for many different productions. The "Splendid Gothic Hall" which features in *Tom Cringle's Log* in all probability also appeared as a "Hall in an Old Town House" in *The Green Bushes*, the "Splendid Mansion of Artois the Death Dealer" in *The Law of Java* and an "Illuminated Hall" in *Ada the Betrayed*. Some kind of stately or ancient interior in fact features in half the playbills. Also in the grand style, though on a slightly smaller scale, is the scene which appears in ten playbills under such descriptions as "An Old-Fashioned Apartment in Lester Hall", "Chamber of the Old Manor House", "An Apartment in Belville Castle" or "Boudoir in Grace Clairville's Mansion". According to Sutton, these representations of gracious living were still the mainstay of the travelling theatres some fifty years later. He felt that no company could afford to be without a "palace set":

> In a particularly well appointed company, this may be supplemented by a panelled oak chamber . . . either of these two scenes will do for Oakdene, Lord Oakleigh's Ancient Home (it is ancient all right), a Mansion of the Idle Rich in Mayfair, a financier's office in New York, the captain's cabin on a French battleship, and other less likely places. I have known the oak-chamber used for the inside of a gasometer with the lights discreetly down. [12]

The most frequently-listed scene, however, is that of a cottage interior which occurs twelve times. A rural village setting comes a close second with eleven. This confirms Michael Booth's observations on the popularity of country locations generally with urban audiences. Jerome K. Jerome found the same fashion prevailing in the 1890's:

> All the virtuous people in the play lived in cottages. I never saw such a run on cottages . . . After one or two more appearances, the cottage became an established favourite with the gallery. So much so, indeed, that when two scenes had passed without it being let down, there were many and anxious enquiries after it, and an earnest hope expressed that nothing serious had happened to it. [13]

Six nautical dramas are featured on these detailed playbills and each of these includes, among other scenes, a ship's deck, a cabin and a general sea view, usually used as a backdrop for shipwrecks or storms. Other scenes which appear on a number of playbills are: the interior of a public house (6), a forest or wood (6), a romantic mountain or cliff view (5), the interior of a hovel or den (presumably not the same as a country cottage) (4), formal gardens (4), a general street scene (3) and a condemned cell (3).

Even allowing for some duplication, an average of nine scene changes per drama would have created a good deal of work in the confined backstage space at Wild's. It is significant that Sam Wild remembers particularly a helpful guest star who would, on occasion "help to pull up a scene" (p. 167). There are also textual references to scene-shifters as permanent members of the company [e.g. p. 55]. When a drama which featured a particularly large number of scenes—such as *Eugene Aram*, which contains three acts and thirteen changes—was being performed, it is probable that only the scenes necessary for each act were hung at one time. During the intervals, while the band played, these scenes were unfastened, rolled up and taken outside to the scenery waggon, the new ones being hung in their place.

In addition to backcloths, set pieces and side flats were used to build up the scenes. Some of these are identified in the inventory drawn up when the business was divided between Sam and Tom Wild in 1856: two cottages, a fireplace, a practicable window piece, rock pieces, ground pieces and a deck piece. One patron of Wild's recalled a practicable bowsprit "which swayed and creaked so naturally that some of us could smell the salt water and tar". [14] This bowsprit played an important part in *The Sea: or, The Ocean Child*, one of the more popular dramas at Old Wild's:

> Sc. VI: A Storm—Part of the Wreck of the Windsor Castle discovered R., the Bowsprit extending sufficiently to realise the two beautiful pictures by Dawe—First a Female struggling with an Infant in her arms, against the raging billows—Second, that of a brave Seaman letting himself down from the Bowsprit, and thus suspended between air and ocean, snatching both the Mother and her Infant from a watery grave.

Although, as we have seen, the stage area in the booth was comparable to that of many major theatres, there were severe limitations on space above, below and behind stage for the installation and operation of machinery. In addition, as noted in Chapter 1, lighting might alternate between candles and gas, thereby necessitating a certain amount of adaptability with regard to some techniques. Notwithstanding these limitations, performances at Old Wild's incorporated quite a considerable range of special effects, some of them surprisingly ambitious.

Among the simpler effects, which would have been within the capabilities of most booth theatres, were thunder and lightning, much used at Wild's for storms and shipwrecks. Thunder could be created by one of two methods: a sheet of iron shaken vigorously, or a "thunder run" —a sloping iron rack down which cannon balls were rolled. Richardson was using the latter method at Bartholomew Fair in 1802 and Billy Purvis paid 2s6d for one of the former in the 1820's, remarking "Nowt like a rattlin' noise, never mind the leetnin' and the bleezes" [15]. The guest star who occasionally helped with the scene changes at Wild's also thoughtfully imparted "most valuable information on the art of manufacturing lightning" (p. 168)—unfortunately not recorded. It could be simulated by a chemical explosion or by an earlier, simpler method:

> A plank must be cut in two along a zig-zag line. It is then placed in the sky over the stage. Another plank, covered in tinsel and carrying a row of candles, is placed behind it. When the lightning is needed, the two halves of the front plank are quickly parted and then re-joined. [16]

Moonlight is frequently called for in melodramatic plots and it is specifically mentioned on ten of the twenty detailed Wild playbills. The lowering and raising of lights necessary for this would have been considerably easier where gas was in use, but was still possible where candles were the only means of illumination. The company with which Edward Stirling travelled in the 1830's provided a very effective moonrise for *Pizarro* by perching a boy with two candles on a ladder behind a gauze-covered hole in the scene, while at the Sans Pareil in 1850, "an awful and convenient darkness" was achieved by the introduction of a plank between the actors and the footlights. In better-equipped booths, footlights could also be lowered into a trough. [17]

The ability to dim some lights and raise others was also necessary for vision scenes. These, in addition, required a special backcloth painted on thinner material. In Wild's production of *Susan Hopley*:

the walls of the apartment seem to dissolve away—and to Susan in her sleep is revealed the vision of the double murder at Upton.
[Playbill, Hull, 21.10.1845]

Another kind of scene which permitted more than one action on stage simultaneously was the built-up set representing several rooms or locations at once. Credit for the invention of this effect is usually given to Edward Fitzball who used it in *Jonathan Bradford* at Sadler's Wells in 1833. Its first recorded use at Old Wild's is for a production of *Jack Sheppard* at Hull on 14 October 1841. The scene in the condemned hold, the playbill declares, "will represent Four Apartments on the Stage at One Time". A more complicated set was created for "The Haunted Room in the Lone House" in *Claude Duval*:

This scene will at one time show the room of the Lone House, the Turret and the River, with the Moon rising—boats passing and re-passing.
[Playbill, Hull, 3.11.1845].

Moving objects feature in several Wild presentations: a full-sized model Indian elephant and "a property serpent gliding down a property tree" are recorded [18]—but mobile boats appear most frequently on the bills. The evidence suggests, indeed, that no fewer than three different kinds of property craft were carried among the set pieces in the scenery van; a gondola or galley, a raft and a fully-rigged sailing ship.

In both *The Aethiop* and *The Black Rover*, a "Splendid Golden Galley" floats across the waves. This boat probably appeared also in *Cherry and Fair Star*: John Coleman recalled such an effect in a production seen in his childhood:

... the attraction of the evening for me was the romantic drama of *Cherry and Fair Star*, with its real golden galley and the mimic waves splashing round it. [19]

A playbill for *The Green Bushes* promises that Miami will be saved from a watery grave "by the timely arrival of a Raft passing down the Mississippi". There is also a raft in *Gallant Paul* on which the hero and heroine are "left to float in solitude amid the howling Tempest, on the wide world of waters". [20]

Both galley and raft would have been on wheels and towed across the stage by means of ropes in the same manner as the "cat chariot" described by Sam in his memoirs (pp. 127–128). The larger, fully-rigged boat—which features in all six of the nautical melodramas for which detailed playbills survive—was also mounted on wheels to enable it to move around in a natural manner. In addition, masts, sails, spars, etc. were fully collapsible, since catastrophic shipwreck was undoubtedly the single most popular sensation scene at Old Wild's: from the evidence it looks very much as though the boat was wrecked in every play in which it appeared.

To create realistic shipwreck scenes, some representation of the ocean is necessary, and indeed some playbills promise: "The Whole of the Stage will be Covered with Water". Sadly, real water is unlikely to have been used. That was the province of permanent theatres with fitted water tanks, like Sadler's Wells. A simpler method of representing stormy seas was with painted canvas sheeting, either agitated by stage hands from the wings or given movement by small boys crawling about underneath. Canvas sheeting would have been used for the raft scene in *Gallant Paul* and for a cabin scene in *The Ocean of Life* where "the rolling waves are seen through the aft windows". For the principal sensation in the latter piece, however, where "the sea covers the wreck", another kind of water effect would have been brought into play. For this several sheets of gauze were stretched across the stage and gradually raised higher and higher, giving the impression that the vessel was sinking. The stage directions for *The Wreck of the Royal George* give a good idea of the effect:

> The waters are seen violently agitated; and are raised one-third above the level of the stage; they are transparent. The sunken vessel is distinctly visible. Sailors are swimming about. [21]

It was this method of simulating deep water which created such a sensation in Boucicault's *Colleen Bawn* first staged in England in 1860. Sam Wild's production of the drama in 1861 won praise for its clever representation of the water-cave scene [22]. It is probable, however, on the evidence of the playbills, that the technique was one with which Old Wild's had been conversant for many years before it was utilised by Boucicault.

In two of the nautical melodramas, *The Mariner's Dream* and *Ben the Boatswain*, the ship goes up in flames before sinking. Buildings on fire provide the other principal special effect, being advertised as the main attraction on four of the playbills. In *The Prophet of the Moor*, the igniting of the mansion at Greville Cross gives rise to a "Grand Conflagration and Terrific Tableaux", while in *Tom Cringle's Log* the scene in which the cottage on the cliff is destroyed by fire is described as "decidedly one of the most effective on the British Stage". *The Aethiop* concludes with "The Conflagration of the Citadel" and *Ada the Betrayed* boasts the double attraction of a blaze at either end: in the opening scene when a baby is "snatched from the devouring element" and in the finale when Mad Maud sets fire to the Lone House [23].

There is little factual information on how these effects were created in the booth but we can be fairly sure that they involved a generous use of coloured fire, a product with which Sam Wild shows himself to be thoroughly familiar. Gunpowder and fireworks, too, were part of the company's stock in trade as evinced by textual descriptions of military spectacles; and a satisfactory finale could be achieved by setting off several explosions simultaneously with the collapse of the burning building. The latter effect could be achieved either by pulling on a rope which toppled the several parts of the specially-constructed set piece or, more simply, by dropping the canvas scene on which the building was painted [24].

The foregoing gives some idea of the effects which were normally in use at Old Wild's. There were undoubtedly others for which details have not survived. Nothing, for example, is known about the techniques used in staging pantomimes, apart from a few tantalising allusions such as that in the *Huddersfield Chronicle* of 28 December 1852 which commented: "the tricks and machinery are well managed" and Sam's reference to children appearing as fairies in a transformation scene, "each reclining on the bosom of a cloud" (p. 142).

It is a little surprising, nevertheless, that no evidence has been unearthed for that standby of the Victorian theatre, the trap. In fact Sam actually seems to emphasise the lack of this particular device when, in describing an 1835 production of *The Bottle Imp*, he says that the descent to pandemonium was "left to the imagination" (p. 31). It is hard to see why Wild's should have done without stage traps, given some of the other theatrical effects which they took the trouble to create. That the trap was used in other booth theatres we know from the evidence of both Mark

Melford and Joe Randel Hodson. The former alludes to a production of Hamlet in which

> . . . the Gravedigger who doubled as the Ghost peered roguishly over the level of the stage into the eyes of a woman spectator clinging to the king pole of the tent, with one foot on the back of the seat, commanding a clear view of the interior of the grave and the layer of grass on which the First Gravedigger was standing . . . [25]

By the time that Hodson was travelling, some forty years later, the booth stage trap had become sophisticated enough to be fitted with all the necessary weights and pulleys to enable demons and spirits to enter with a leap [26].

The most likely explanation is that one or more forms of stage trap were taken for granted at Wild's as in other theatres and not considered worthy of especial notice. There are, after all, dramas listed in the repertoire which depend on stage traps as part of the plot. *The Corsican Brothers*, for example, was brought out "with new and startling mechanical effects" (p. 151). This can only refer to the Corsican Trap with its gliding ghost, since the only other major effect is the vision scene which, though essential to the plot, would hardly be described as "new and startling". Another piece, *Bill Jones: or, The Spectre by Sea and Land*, hinges (to use a particularly apposite term) from start to finish on vampire traps, Bill's ghost appearing through a Vampire Tree, a Vampire Garden Chair and even a Vampire Coffin:

> (*Bill's Spectre rises from the Coffin and sinks.*)
> HARRY   I cannot believe my eyes—it must be some trick!
> (*Pulls coffin over, showing bottom to audience—*
> *empty—in panic places coffin as before. The*
> *Spectre of Bill arises instantly. Harry starts*
> *back to R. corner, afraid.*)
> BILL   Repent, atone, pray and be forgiven.
> (*Sinks again. Business as before.*)

It would, of course, be possible for a booth to present such dramas with the main effects either cut out altogether or represented in a fairly basic way. A comparison was therefore made between the original playtexts and the details contained in the Wild playbills to see how far the company endeavoured to adhere to the original directions.

The detailed Wild playbills may be divided into those which contain a large amount of scenic detail and description but little in the way of notable effects, and those which rely chiefly on technical effects to attract the audience. Four in the former category, advertising *Eugene Aram*, *Grace Clairville*, *Peter Bell the Waggoner* and *Susan Hopley*, were compared with the original playtexts. In each case the descriptions of scenes were found to be virtually identical, even to a romantic landscape with water mill in *Peter Bell* and a house interior in *Susan Hopley*:

> Kitchen in Parliament-street; the area with palisades and steps leading to the street seen through the window [Playbill, Hull, 21.10.1845]

This could merely mean, of course, that the scenic descriptions were simply copied direct from the text on to the playbills and although this confirms that Wild's worked from the offical playtexts and not from pirated versions, the playbills cannot really be relied upon to give any real information about the standard and extent of the scenery carried. Indeed, there is no way of ascertaining whether all the scenes listed on the playbills actually made an appearance or not. Wilkie Collins found a disparity in this respect between expectation and experience at a booth performance:

> In act the second, the first scene was described on the bills as Temple Bar by moonlight. Neither Bar nor moonlight appeared whenn the curtain rose—so we took both for granted and fixed our minds on the story. [27]

This reservation, however, could be made about almost any theatre, permanent or otherwise, in a period which lacks photographic evidence. The scenery at Wild's may well not have been as spectacular or lavish as that displayed at the major London theatres, but enough evidence has been unearthed to show that it was regarded as of considerable import- ance. We should also bear in mind the significant fact that the waggon which was specially built to transport the scenery was christened the "colossal" van (p. 170).

When we come to a comparison of technical effects, on the other hand, enough variation can be found to show that in this field at least Wild's did not advertise effects it could not hope to reproduce. Acts II and III of *Gallant Paul* may be taken as an example. The original stage directions for the finale of Act II read:

> *Diorama of the Departure of the Raven from Portsmouth Harbour —a Mechanical Vessel, fully built and rigged, tacks about and ultimately sails off L.U.E.—the Diorama works on and discovers the main ocean by sunset.*

Clearly a diorama was not something which could be easily fitted into the booth for a single performance, as the Wild playbill advertises a slightly simpler, although still fairly ambitious, spectacle:

THE RAVEN IN FULL SAIL
Which will Tack from One Side of the Stage
to the Other.
The Main Ocean by Moonlight.

Act III shows a more interesting and creative variation by Wild's. In the original text, the act opens on the deck of a ship. A storm blows up and clouds descend. When they ascend, the ship's deck has given place to the open sea with the survivors clinging to a piece of wreckage. On the Wild playbill, the act opens in a similar manner, but as the storm blows up, lifeboats are brought alongside to rescue the crew. The scene then changes and the audience are given another chance to see the Raven in full sail before she is struck by lightning, thus clearing the way for a

DREADFUL SHIPWRECK
with
Horrible Screams of the Crew
Preservation of Paul and Mary by means of a Raft . . .
[Playbill, Hull, 23.10.1844]

This is an obvious instance of the script being altered to include effects which were within the capacity of the company. *Tom Cringle* provides another example. The original stage directions call for the brief app-

earance of a sailing ship which the wreckers are trying to lure to her
doom: the hero, however, exclaims:

> No! up thou to yonder turret top, extinguish the false beacon,
> while I to the Bay and set in flames the old straw cottage on the cliff
> —so the ship may tack to whither she may ride in safety ...

When this piece was brought out at Wild's, however, it appears that while
the stage manager was quite willing to stage the spectacle of the burning
cottage, he was reluctant to forgo the usual maritime catastrophe to which
his audiences had become accustomed over the years. Despite the best
efforts of the hero, therefore, and the wholehearted cooperation of the
cottage, the scene ends, satisfactorily, with the spectacular "Wreck of an
East India Merchantman!" [28]

Overall the comparison of playbills with original texts shows that as
far as possible the stage directions were followed, only those effects being
omitted which were clearly beyond the scope of the portable theatre,
being dependent on such facilities as extensive flying space or complex
machinery. It is significant that when Wild's produced a version of W.
T. Moncrieff's Indian spectacle, this was brought out under its alternative title of *The Rajah's Daughter* and not the original, which was *The
Cataract of the Ganges*. A sensation scene in which the heroine rode a
horse up a foaming cataract of real water was not within the capacity of
a travelling company, even one so ambitious as Old Wild's. Such
omissions and adaptations, however, only serve to emphasise how much
was in fact achieved by Old Wild's in the way of special effects. The
spectacular finale of *The Black Rover: or, The Rock of Death*, presented
to a presumably appreciative Drypool audience on 19 August 1844,
deserves to be reproduced here as a final tribute to one of the great
Victorian travelling theatres:

> Interior of a Magnificent Saloon. Splendid Banquet!
> Around are Vases of Flowers and Other Decorations.
> GRAND MORICIAN SYMBOL DANCE!
> Treachery of Quito—"Ha, what do I behold?"—
> The Spectre of the Murdered Duca is Seen
> The Vases on each side Sink and discover
> Groups of Spectres in various Attitudes.

Fiends burst forth and point to the different groups
SURROUNDED BY FLAMES OF
GREEN AND RED FIRE!
Which casts a Supernatural Light over the Entire Picture
Terrific Combat and
DESTRUCTION OF THE ROCK OF DEATH!!!

REFERENCES

1. Rowell, G., *The Victorian Theatre*, 1956, 14.
2. Egan, P., *The Life of an Actor*, 1825. "Peter Paterson", *op. cit.* Dickens, C., e.g. "Greenwich Fair" in *Sketches by Boz*, 1836. Booth, M., *English Melodrama*, 1956, 55.
3. Mayhew, H., *op. cit.*, 126 & 139; Melford, M., *op. cit.*, 18.
4. For example, 75 & 93; 58.
5. Jackson, B., "Barnstorming Days" in *Studies in English Theatre History*, 1952, 114–123.
6. O. W., 21, 89, 115, 172, 232, 234.
7. O. W., 25, 56, 140.
8. Playbill collection, Hull Central Library.
9. *The Theatrical Repertory*, No. XXII, 15.2.1802. Green, W., *op. cit.*, 280.
10. Dobson, T., in the *Blackburn Times*, 4.1.1902. *Chambers' Journal, op. cit.*
11. Southern, R., *The Victorian Theatre*, 1970. 31. *Chambers' Journal, op. cit.*; Jackson, B., *op. cit.*; Sutton, G., *Fish and Actors*, NY 1925, 11–12.
12. Playbill Collection, Hull Central Library. Sutton, G., *op. cit.*, 12–13.
13. Jerome, J. K., *On the Stage and Off*, 1885, 59–60.
14. O. W., 134; Dobson, T., *op. cit.*
15. Mahard, M. R., *op. cit.*, 211; Arthur, T., *op. cit.*, 53.
16. Sabbattini, N., *Pratica di Fabricar Scene*, 1638, Vol. II, quoted in Gascoigne, B., *World Theatre*, 1968, 210.
17. Stirling, E., *op. cit.*; Collins, W., *op. cit.*
18. O. W., 110 & 162; also *Preston Herald*, 17.5.1856.
19. Coleman, J. C., *Fifty Years of an Actor's Life*, 1904, Vol. I, 76.
20. Playbills dated 30.10.1845 and 23.10.1844, Hull Central Library.
21. Playbill dated 21.10.1841, Hull Central Library; playbill dated 29.6.1842, Wakefield Central Library.
22. *Era*, 27.10.1861.
23. Playbill collections, Hull & Wakefield Central Libraries.
24. See, for example, p. 31.
25. Melford, M., *op. cit.*, 31.
26. Hodson, J. R., *op. cit.*
27. Collins, W., *op. cit.*, 123.
28. Playbill dated 19.10.1842, Hull Central Library.

APPENDIX A

CHRONOLOGICAL CHART OF OLD WILD's TRAVELS

NOTE. The information given in the text is scanty, particularly in the case of the earlier years. The details set out below have been gleaned, for the most part, from the pages of *The Era* but also from local newspapers, playbills, and other contemporary evidence. Only dates for which there is definite evidence are recorded.

	1831	1932	1833	1834
Jan.	Halifax		Rotherham	
Feb.				
Mar.				
April				
May				
June				
July	Wakefield			
Aug.				
Sept.				
Oct.	Nottingham		Nottingham	
Nov.				
Dec.		Rotherham		

	1835	1836	1837	1838	1839	1840	1841	1842
Jan.			Preston		Huddersfield			Bradford
Feb.			Preston		Huddersfield			Bradford
Mar.			Blackburn		Huddersfield			
April	Blackburn				Blackburn			
May								
June		Bradford	Halifax	Halifax		Wakefield		
July								Wakefield
Aug.								
Sept.	Holbeck							
Oct.	Leeds						Nottingham/Hull	Hull
Nov.	Leeds						Bradford	Bradford
Dec.		Preston		Bradford/Hudd.			Bradford	Bradford

1843		1844		1845		1846	
Jan.	Bradford	Jan.	Bradford	Jan.		Jan.	
Feb.	Bradford	Feb.	Bradford	Feb.		Feb.	
Mar.		Mar.	Bradford	Mar.		Mar.	
April		April		April		April	
May		May		May		May	
June		June		June	Sheffield	June	Lancaster
July		July		July	Leeds	July	Leeds
Aug.	Drypool	Aug.	Drypool	Aug.	Drypool	Aug.	Drypool
Sept.		Sept.		Sept.		Sept.	Beverley
Oct.	Hull	Oct.	Hull	Oct.	Hull	Oct.	Hull
Nov.	Bradford	Nov.		Nov.		Nov.	
Dec.	Bradford	Dec.	Bradford	Dec.		Dec.	

Also visited pre-1849, although exact dates not known: Knottingley, Manchester, Newark.

1847		1848		1849	
Jan.		Jan.		Jan.	
Feb.		Feb.		Feb.	
Mar.	Blackburn	Mar.		Mar.	Bolton
April		April		April	Blackburn
May		May	Leeds	May	Preston
June		June		June	Preston
July		July		July	Lancaster/Leeds
Aug.		Aug.		Aug.	Kendal
Sept.		Sept.		Sept.	Penrith

1847 cont.		1848 cont.		1849 cont.	
Oct.	Hull	Oct.		Oct.	Appleby
Nov.		Nov.	Bury	Nov.	Carlisle
Dec.		Dec.	Heywood	Dec.	Carlisle

1850		1851		1852	
Jan.	Carlisle	Jan.	Huddersfield	Jan.	Keighley
Feb.	Carlisle	Feb.	Huddersfield	Feb.	Keighley
Mar.	Wigton	Mar.	Cleckheaton	Mar.	
April	Carlisle/Maryport	April	Keighley	April	Colne
May	Whitehaven	May	Huddersfield	May	Burnley
June	Preston/Halifax	June	Holmfirth/Bradford	June	Skipton/Bradford
July		July	Halifax	July	Halifax/Leeds
Aug.		Aug.	Cleckheaton	Aug.	
Sept.	Holbeck	Sept.	Armley/Holbeck	Sept.	
Oct.	Halifax	Oct.		Oct.	Halifax
Nov.	Huddersfield	Nov.	Dewsbury	Nov.	Wakefield
Dec.	Huddersfield	Dec.		Dec.	Dewsbury

1853		1854		1855	
Jan.	Ashton under Lyme	Jan.	Bury	Jan.	Bury
Feb.	Ashton under Lyme	Feb.	Bury	Feb.	Bury
Mar.	Keighley	Mar.		Mar.	Bury
April		April	Rochdale	April	Blackburn
May		May	Blackburn	May	Blackburn
June	Ripon	June		June	Halifax
July	Wakefield	July	Leeds	July	
Aug.	Dewsbury	Aug.		Aug.	

1853 cont.

Sept.	Armley
Oct.	Dewsbury
Nov.	Bury
Dec.	Bury

1856

Jan.	Dewsbury
Feb.	Dewsbury
Mar.	Blackburn
April	Blackburn
May	Preston
June	Skipton/Keighley
July	Halifax/Barnsley
Aug.	Horton
Sept.	Armley/Holbeck
Oct.	Halifax
Nov.	Halifax
Dec.	Dewsbury

1859

Jan.	Burnley
Feb.	Burnley
Mar.	Burnley
April	Accrington
May	Blackburn
June	Preston/Halifax
July	Wakefield/Leeds/Dewsb'y

1854 cont.

Sept.	
Oct.	Halifax
Nov.	
Dec.	Bury

1857

Jan.	Dewsbury
Feb.	Dewsbury
Mar.	Dewsbury
April	Blackburn
May	Blackburn
June	Preston
July	Halifax/Pontefract
Aug.	Dews/Brighse/Pudsey
Sept.	Armley/Holbeck
Oct.	Halifax
Nov.	Dewsbury
Dec.	Halifax/Wigan

1860

Jan.	Keighley/Skipton
Feb.	Blackburn
Mar.	Blackburn
April	Blackburn
May	Accrington/Preston
June	Wigan/St. Helen's/Bolton/Leigh/Bury
July	Heywood/Rochdale/Oldham/Huddersfield

1855 cont.

Sept.	Armley
Oct.	Halifax
Nov.	Halifax
Dec.	Wakefield/Dewsbury

1858

Jan.	Wigan
Feb.	Wigan
Mar.	Wigan
April	Blackburn
May	Preston
June	Halifax
July	Dewsbury
Aug.	Pudsey
Sept.	Armley/Holbeck
Oct.	Halifax
Nov.	Burnley
Dec.	Burnley

1859 cont.

Aug.	Hunslet
Sept.	Armley
Oct.	Pudsey
Nov.	Keighley
Dec.	Keighley

1860 cont.

Aug.	Brighouse/Hunslet
Sept.	Holbeck
Oct.	Blackburn
Nov.	Blackburn
Dec.	Blackburn

1861

Jan.	Blackburn
Feb.	Accrington
Mar.	
April	
May	Preston
June	Lancaster/Halifax
July	Wakefield
Aug.	Brighouse
Sept.	
Oct.	Wakefield
Nov.	Wakefield
Dec.	Huddersfield

1862

Jan.	Huddersfield
Feb.	Huddersfield
Mar.	Huddersfield
April	Huddersfield
May	
June	
July	Wakefield
Aug.	
Sept.	
Oct.	
Nov.	Huddersfield
Dec.	Huddersfield

1863

Jan.	Huddersfield
Feb.	Huddersfield
Mar.	Huddersfield
April	Huddersfield
May	Huddersfield
June	Elland
July	Wakefield/Knottingley
Aug.	Hunslet
Sept.	Armley/Holbeck
Oct.	Keighley
Nov.	Keighley
Dec.	(S.W. in York Jail)

1864

(S.W. in _ail)

Jan.	
Feb.	
Mar.	
April	Shipley
May	Bradford
June	Halifax

1865

Jan.	Dewsbury
Feb.	Cleckheaton/Brighouse
Mar.	Heckmondwike
April	
May	Brighouse/Shelf
June	Halifax

	1864 cont.	1865 cont.
July	Dewsbury	
Aug.	Hunslet	
Sept.	Armley/Holbeck	
Oct.	Dewsbury	
Nov.	Dewsbury	
Dec.	Dewsbury	

APPENDIX B

LIST OF PLAYS PERFORMED BY OLD WILD'S

The plays are listed alphabetically with details in the following order: Title under which the piece was played by Wild's; description (if known) given for the piece by Wild's or other contemporary source; source of information; date of first recorded performance by Wild's; author, date of first London performance and classification, according to Allardyce Nicoll (preceded by title, if this differs significantly from that used by Wild's). It should be noted that the date of first recorded performance of a piece by Wild's is unlikely, in most cases, to be the first time the piece was ever played by the company.

Ada the Betrayed; or, The Murder at the Old Smithy.
"Admired Drama". "For the first time this season. Now performing in London in almost every theatre." (Playbill.) Hull, 29.10.1844. (Not listed in Nicoll; printed in *Oxberry's Budget* 21.1.1844, and described as being "founded on the popular work of that name by E. Edwards Esq.".)

Aethiop, The; or, The Child of the Desert.
"New and Gorgeous Spectacle." (Playbill.) Hull, 19.10.1843. (Nicoll: W. Dimond, 6.10.1812, MD.)

Africans, The; or, Love and Duty.
"Melo-Drama". (Playbill.) Holbeck, Sept. 1859. (Nicoll: G. Colman the Younger, 29.7.1808.)

Aladdin; or, The Wonderful Lamp.
"Pantomime". (*Era*, 13.1.1850.) Carlisle, 12.1.1850. (Nicoll: numerous versions listed from 1780 onwards.)

Armstrong the Shipwright.
(*Era*, 14.8.64.) Dewsbury, August 1864. (Nicoll: J. T. Haines, 2.9.1839, D.)

Bandit Merchant, The; or, The Maid of the Inn.
"Drama". (*Burnley Advertiser*, 12.2.59.) Burnley, 12.2.1859. (Nicoll: *The Maid of Genoa; or, The Bandit Merchant*; J. Farrell, 26.6.1820.)

Bathing.
"Farce". (*Era*, 26.8.49.) Kendal, August 1849. (Nicoll: J. Bruton, 31.1.1842.)

Bath Road, The: or, The Biter Bit.
"Laughable Farce". (Text, p. 63.) Bradford, Jan. 1844. (Nicoll: J. Poole, 14.10.1830, Int.)

Battle of Austerlitz, The.
(*Era*, 8.12.61.) Wakefield, 30.11.1861. (Nicoll: *Austerlitz; or, The Soldier's Bride*; J. T. Haines, 26.9.1831, MD.) See also *The Wars of Napoleon.*

Battle of Kalafat, The.
"A local drama, based on the late stirring events, representing the Russian and Turkish war at the Battle of Kalafat". (*Era*, 23.4.54.) Blackburn, April 1854. (Not listed in Nicoll; probably a company dramatisation.)

Battle of the Alma, The.
"Drama". (Text, pp. 117–18.) Bury, Jan. 1855. Written especially for Wild's by C. R. Somerset. (Nicoll lists a version by an unknown author at Astley's on 23.10.54 and the next, by J. H. Stocqueler, on 26.2.55. D.)

Battle of Trafalgar, The.
(*Era*, 2.3.51.) Huddersfield, Feb. 1851. (Nicoll lists two versions, both by unknown authors, 14.4.1806 and 7.6.1824.)

Battle of Waterloo, The.
"Dramatic Spectacle". (*Era*, 3.2.50.) Carlisle, Jan. 1850. (Nicoll: J. H. Amherst, 19.4.1824, Spec.)

Bear Hunters, The.
"Drama". (Text, p. 66.) Bradford, 18.3.1844. (Nicoll: J. B. Buckstone, 25.4.1825, MD.)

Beggar's Petition, The; or, A Father's Love and a Mother's Care.
"Popular Drama". (*Wigan Observer*, 19.12.57.) Wigan, Dec. 1857. (Nicoll: G. Dibdin Pitt, 18.10.1841, D.) See also *Jane Brightwell.*

Belphegor the Mountebank.
(Text, p. 115.) Bury, 17.1.1855. (Nicoll: B. N. Webster, 13.1.1851, D.)

Ben Brace; or, The Last of Nelson's Agamemnons.
(Text, p. 62.) Date of first perf. not known; printed in *Oxberry's* Budget
25.12.1843. (Nicoll: J. S. Faucit, 6.6.1836. MD.)

Ben Liel; or, The Son of Night.
"Sensational drama". "First night in England." (Text, p. 223.)
Dewsbury, 25.11.1864. (Nicoll: W. Travers, 4.5.1857.)

Ben the Boatswain; or, The Burning Ship.
"Nautical Drama". (Playbill.) Wakefield, 25.6.1842. (Nicoll: ... *or,
Sailors' Sweethearts*; T. E. Wilks, 19.8.1839, D.)

Bill Jones; or, The Spectre by Sea and Land.
(*Era*, 13.11.53.) Dewsbury, Nov. 1853. (Nicoll: John Kerr, 1834 or J. H.
Amherst, date unknown.)

Black Doctor, The.
"Romantic Drama". (Text, p. 168.) Burnley, Jan. 1859. (Nicoll: T.
Archer, 9.11.1846, D.)

Black-Ey'd Susan; or, All in the Downs.
"Nautical Drama". (Text, p. 21.) Date of first perf. not known, but in
repertoire c. 1832. (Nicoll: D. W. Jerrold, 8.6.1829, MD.)

Black Reefer, The; or, A New Tale of the Sea.
(Text, p. 62.) Date of first perf. not known; printed in *Oxberry's* Budget
16.10.1843. (Nicoll notes this as originally entitled *The Contraband
Captain*; M. Corri, 26.2.1835, MD.)

Black Rover, The; or, The Rock of Death.
"Romantic Drama". "For the First Time Here ... As Acted for Upwards
of One Hundred Nights at the Surrey Theatre." (Playbill.) Drypool,
19.8.1844. (Nicoll: E. R. Lancaster, 13.1.1840.)

Blindman's Buff; or, Who Pays the Piper?
"Laughable Farce". (Playbill.) Hull, 15.10.1841. (Nicoll: T. J. Dibdin,
1.2.1802, OF.)

Bloomers!
"Farce". (*Era*, 16.5.52.) Burnley, 12.5.1852. (Nicoll: C. R. Somerset,
13.10.1851, F.)

Blue Beard.
(*Era*, 13.1.50.) Carlisle, 12.1.1850. (Nicoll: G. Colman the Younger, 16.1.1798, MD.)

Bohemians, The; or, The Rogues of Paris.
"For the first time". (Text, p. 66.) Bradford, 18.3.1844. (Nicoll: E. Stirling, 16.11.1843, D.)

Bombastes Furioso.
"Laughable Farce". (Playbill.) Hull, 29.10.1845. (Nicoll: C. Selby, 8.6.1842, F.)

Boots at the Swan.
"Laughable Farce". (Playbill.) Hull, 29.10.1845. (Nicoll: C. Selby, 8.6.1842, F.)

Bottle, The; or, The Life and Death of a Drunkard.
"Moral drama". (*Era*, 24.6.49.) Preston, 20.6.1849. (Nicoll: T. P. Taylor, 18.10.1847, D.)

Bottle Imp, The; or, The Fiend and the Sorcerer.
"Romantic Drama". (Text, p. 27.) Leeds, 25.11.1835. (Nicoll: R. B. Peake, 7.7.1828, MD.)

Bound 'Prentice to a Waterman; or, The Death Dealer of Batavia!
"Nautical Drama". (Playbill.) Hull, 8.10.1842. (Nicoll: . . . or, The Flower of Woolwich; A. V. Campbell, 19.7.1836, D.) See also *The Law of Java.*

Bradford Cobbler, The.
"Laughable Farce". (Playbill.) Bradford, 2.3.1844. (Not listed in Nicoll; a farce called *The Wakefield Cobbler* was played by a travelling company at Hartlepool in 1844.)

Breakers Ahead; or, The Shipwreck of the Spanker.
(Text, p. 59.) Date of first perf. not known, but in repertoire by the winter of 1841–2. (Nicoll: J. T. Haines, 27.3.1837, D.)

Break o'Morn; or, The Dark Hour.
"Sensation drama" (Text, p. 201.) Huddersfield, 9.2.1863. (Nicoll: unknown author, 23.7.1862.) Wild says this was "written expressly" for James Holloway.

Broken-Hearted Father, The.
(*Era,* 28.11.58.) Burnley, Nov. 1858. This is probably a version of *The Lear of Private Life*—see below. See also *Smiles and Tears.*

Brutus; or, The Fall of Tarquin.
"Tragedy". (*Oxberry's Budget,* 26.2.44.) Bradford, 13.2.1844. (Nicoll: J. H. Payne, 3.12.1818, T.)

Brigand, The.
(Text, p. 117.) Bury, c. Feb. 1855. (Nicoll: D. W. Osbaldistone, 18.11.1830, D.)

Buried Alive!
"Farce". (Playbill.) Wakefield, 25.6.1842. (Nicoll: possibly *The Caffres; or, Buried Alive*; E. J. Eyre, 2.6.1802, C.O.)

California; or, The Land of Gold.
(*Era,* 17.6.49.) Preston, June 1849. (Not listed in Nicoll; a piece entitled *Gold Seekers of California* was presented at the Theatre Royal, Hull, 17.2.1849.)

Captain's Not A-Miss, The!
"Farce". (Text, p. 109.) Ripon, 10.6.1853. (Nicoll: T. E. Wilks, 18.4.1836, O.F.)

Caravan Driver and his Dog, The.
"Drama". (*Era,* 7.1.55.) Bury, 1.1.1855. (Nicoll: *The Caravan; or, The Driver and his Dog*; Frederic Reynolds, 5.12.1803, MD.)

Carpenter of Rouen, The.
(*Era,* 15.2.57.) Dewsbury, 11.2.1857. (Nicoll: J. Jones, 24.6.44, D.)

Cartouche.
(*Era,* 15.3.63.) Huddersfield, 12.3.1863. (Nicoll: several versions listed from 1840 onwards, MD.)

Castle Spectre, The; or, The Haunted Oratory.
"Lewis's Beautiful Play". (Playbill.) Hull, 29.10.1847. (Nicoll: M. G. Lewis, 14.12.1797, MD.)

Catherine Howard; or, The Tomb! The Throne! and The Scaffold!
"Romantic Drama". (Text, p. 169.) Burnley, Feb. 1859. Written by John Coleman. (Nicoll: unknown author, Bolton, 16.7.1858.)

Chaos is Come Again; or, The Race-Ball.
"Farce". (*Oxberry's Budget*, 26.2.44.) Bradford, 16.2.44. (Nicoll: J. M. Morton, 19.11.1838, F.)

Cherry and Fair Star; or, The Children of Cyprus.
Advertised at different times as "Interesting Drama" and "Pantomime". (*Wakefield Journal*, 3.7.40.) Wakefield, 3.7.1840. (Nicoll: unknown author 8.4.1822, MD.)

Cherry Bounce.
"Farce". (Text, p. 16.) Halifax, c. 1825. (Nicoll: R. J. Raymond, 27.8.1821, F.)

Children of the Wood, The.
"Pantomime". (*Era*, 20.5.49.) Blackburn, 13.5.1849. (Nicoll lists various versions from 1793 onwards.)

Christmas in the Olden Times.
"Popular Drama". (*Burnley Advertiser*, 24.12.58.) Burnley, 24.12.1858. (Not listed in Nicoll.)

Claude Duval, the Highwayman of 1666; or, The Lone House in White-friars!
"Drama". (Playbill.) Hull, 3.11.1845. (Nicoll: J. T. Haines, 3.5.1841, D)

Colleen Bawn, The; or, The Brides of Garryowen.
"Drama". (*Era*, 27.10.61.) Wakefield, 21.10.1861. (Nicoll: D. Boucicault; first perf. in England, 10.9.1860, D.)

Come Whoam To Thi' Childer An' Me!
Advertised as "Great Lancashire Drama" and "Domestic Drama". (Text, p. 139.) Barnsley, 5.8.1856. Written by C. R. Somerset. (Not listed in Nicoll.)

Convict Ship, The.
(*Burnley Advertiser*, 19.3.59.) Burnley, 19.3.1859. Probably *The Floating Beacon*—see below.

Corsican Brothers, The.
"Popular Drama". (Text, p. 151.) Dewsbury, 30.1.1857. (Nicoll: D. Boucicault, 24.2.1852, D.)

Cut for Partners.
"Farce". (*Era*, 2.9.49.) Kendal, 29.8.1849. (Nicoll: J. Bruton, 13.5.1844, F.)

Damon and Pythias.
(*Era*, 20.2.59.) Burnley, Feb. 1859. (Nicoll: J. Banim and R. L. Sheil, 28.5.1821, T.)

Dan and Pompey.
"Farce". (*Era*, 20.1.61.) Blackburn, 16.1.1861. Also advertised as *Don and Pampy*. (Not listed in Nicoll.)

Dark Spirit of the Dismal Swamp, The.
(*Era*, 20.5.49.) Blackburn, 11.5.1849. (Nicoll suggests *Nick of the Woods; or, The Altar of Revenge*; J. T. Haines, 1839, MD.) N.B. This piece should not be confused with *Dred: A Tale of the Dismal Swamp*, listed below.

Day After the Wedding, The.
"Laughable Farce". (*Oxberry's Budget*, 28.2.44.) Bradford, 13.2.1844. (Nicoll: M. T. Kemble, 18.5.1808, Int.)

Day at Madrid, A.
"Laughable Farce". (Playbill.) Hull, 22.10.1845. (Not listed in Nicoll.)

Days of Oliver Cromwell, The.
(*Huddersfield Chronicle*, 16.11.50.) Huddersfield, 23.11.1850. (Nicoll: unknown author, 4.10.1847.)

Deaf as a Post.
"Laughable Farce". (Playbill.) Hull, 23.10.1844. (Nicoll: J. Poole, 15.2.1823, F.)

Dick Tarleton.
(Text, p. 140.) Halifax, Oct. or Nov. 1856. Dramatised by a member of the company—possibly Mellers. (Nicoll lists a version by an unknown author, 11.6.1856.)

Dick Whittington and his Cat.
"New Comic Pantomime". (Playbill.) Hull, 31.10.1842. (Numerous versions listed in Nicoll, but none early enough.)

Did You Ever Send Your Wife to Beverley?
"Farce". (Playbill.) Hull, 19.10.1846.

Did You Ever Send Your Wife to Gretna Green?
"Farce". (*Era*, 20.1.50.) Carlisle, 16.1.1850.
(Both local versions of *Did You Ever Send Your Wife to Camberwell?* J.
S. Coyne, 16.3.1846, F.)

Dogs of the Plantation, The; or, A British Sailor in his Glory.
"Interesting drama". (*Preston Guardian*, 3.6.57.) Preston, June 1857.
This may possibly be a version of *The Slave's Revenge; or, The Planter
and his Dogs*—see below.

Dogs of the Regiment, The.
"Drama". (*Era*, 17.6.55.) Blackburn, 11.6.1855. (Not listed in Nicoll.)

Dog(s) of the Wave, The.
(*Era*, 9.6.50.) Preston, 3.6.1850. See *The Pirate Ship.*

Domestic Economy.
"Farce". (*Era*, 29.9.61.) Wakefield, 28.9.1861. (Nicoll: M. Lemon,
8.11.1849, F.)

Don Caesar de Bazan.
"Farce". (Text, p. 110.) Dewsbury, 28.10.1853. (Nicoll: G. A. A'Beckett
and M. Lemon, 8.10.1844, D.)

Don Juan.
Described at different times as "Serious Pantomime" and "Burlesque".
(*Era*, 8.12.50.) Huddersfield, 3.12.1850. (Nicoll: J. B. Buckstone,
24.6.1830, Ba.)

The Dream at Sea; or, The Haunted Cave.
"Beautiful and Pathetic Drama". (Playbill.) Hull, 1.11.1843. (Nicoll: J.
B. Buckstone, 23.11.1835, D.)

Dred: A Tale of the Dismal Swamp.
(*Era*, 8.2.57.) Dewsbury, 2.2.1857. (Nicoll: W. E. Suter, 10/1856, D.0

Druid's Stone, The.
(*Era*, 1.12.50.) Huddersfield, 25.11.1850. See *The Prophet of the Moor.*

Dumb Man of Manchester, The; or, The Felon Heir.
"Beautiful Domestic Drama". (Playbill.) Hull, 21.10.1842. (Nicoll: B. Rayner, 25.9.1837, D.)

England, Ireland and Australia.
(*Era*, 9.6.61.) Lancaster, 5.6.1861. (Not listed in Nicoll; nearest is *Give a Dog a Bad Name; or, England and Australia*; G. H. Lewes, 18.4.1854, F.)

Esmeralda, the Gypsy Girl; or, The Deformed of Notre Dame.
"Favourite Play". (Playbill.) Drypool, 15.8.1845. (Nicoll: E. Fitzball, 14.4.1834, MD.)

Eugene Aram; or, The Murder at St. Robert's Cave.
"Domestic Drama". (Playbill.) Hull, 1.11.1844. (Nicoll: W. T. Moncrieff, 8.2.1832, MD.)

Eustace Baudin; or, A Dark Page in a Poor Man's History.
"Domestic Drama". (*Burnley Advertiser*, 15.1.59.) Burnley, 17.1.1859. (Nicoll: J. Courtney, 30.1.1854.)

Every Inch a Sailor; or, The Ocean of Life.
"New and highly affecting Nautical Melodrama". (Playbill.) Halifax, 28.6.1837. First perf. (Nicoll: (title reversed) J. T. Haines, 4.4.1836.) See also *The Ocean of Life*.

Factory Boy, The.
"Drama". (Playbill.) Wakefield, July 1842. (Nicoll: J. T. Haines, 8.6.1840, DD.)

Fair Rosamond, According to the History of England.
(*Era*, 20.5.49.) Blackburn, 11.5.1849. (Nicoll: T. P. Taylor, 1838, Bsq.)

Faith, Hope and Charity.
"Great London Drama". (*Burnley Advertiser*, 4.12.58.) Burnley, Dec. 1858. (Nicoll: E. L. Blanchard, 7.7.1845, DD.)

Fall of Delhi, The; or, The Cawnpore Massacre.
(*Preston Herald*, 29.5.58.) Preston, May 1858. See *The Storming of Delhi*.

Fall of Sebastopol, The; or, The Allies in the East.
"New patriotic drama". (Text, pp. 123–4.) Halifax, 14.11.1855. Written

for Wild's by Somerset. (Nicoll lists a version by an unknown author at Astley's, 24.9.1855, Spec.)

Family Jars; or, Who's the Master?
"Farce". (*Era*, 8.7.49.) Lancaster, 29.6.1849. (Nicoll: J. Lunn, 28.6.1822, O.F.)

Farmer Highwayman, The.
(*Era*, 23.2.62.) Huddersfield, 17.2.1862. (Not listed in Nocoll.)

Father and Son.
(*Era*, 2.9.49.) Kendal, 27.8.1849. (Nicoll: E. Fitzball, 28.2.1825, MD.)

Ferryman and his Dogs, The.
(*Era*, 22.8.58.) Dewsbury, 18.8.1858. (Not listed in Nicoll, but possibly *The Ferryman of the Lone Hut*, T. P. Taylor, 27.11.1843.)

Fiend of the Lighthouse, The.
"Romantic Drama". (Playbill.) Hull, 27.10.1843. (Nicoll: *The Monster of the Eddystone; or, The Lighthouse Keepers*; G. Dibdin Pitt, 7.4.1834, MD.)

Flat and Sharp.
"Laughable Farce". (Playbill.) Hull, 20.10.1842. (Nicoll (title reversed): D. Lawler, 4.8.1813, OF.) See also *Sharp and Flat*.

Floating Beacon, The; or, The Wild Woman of the Wreck.
(Text, pp. 10, 24, 35.) Date of first perf. not known, but in repertoire c. 1830. (Nicoll: . . . *or, The Norwegian Wreckers*; E. Fitzball, 19.4.1824.)

Flowers of the Forest, The.
(*Era*, 6.5.49.) Blackburn, 2.5.1849. (Nicoll: J. B. Buckstone, 11.3.1847, MD.)

Forest of Bondy, The; or, The Dog of Montargis.
(Text, p. 74.) In repertoire c. 1845. (Nicoll (title reversed): T. J. Dibdin, 6.10.1814, Spec.; also W. Barrymore, 30.9.1814, MD.)

Fortune's Frolic; or, The Ploughman Turned Lord.
"Farce". (*Theatrical Times*, 11.11.1848.) Heywood, c. Nov. 1848. (Nicoll: J. J. Allingham, 25.5.1799, F.)

Four Mowbrays, The.
(Text, p. 202.) Huddersfield, March 1863. (Nicoll: unknown author, 6.10.1851, D.)

Fourteen Years of a Transport's Life.
(*Era*, 27.5.49.) Blackburn, 19.5.1849. (Not listed in Nicoll; a travelling company performed *The Unknown; or, Seven Years of a Transport's Life* at Hartlepool in 1848.)

Frankenstein; or, The Man and the Monster.
"Romantic Drama". (Playbill.) Hull, 19.10.1842. (Nicoll: H. M. Milner, 18.10.1823, MD.)

French Conscription, The.
"Extravaganza". (*Burnley Advertiser*, 5.2.59.) Burnley, 5.2.1859. (Not listed in Nicoll.) Possibly *The Weaver of Lyons*—see below.

Gallant Paul; or, The Wreck of the Raven.
"Nautical Drama". (Text, p. 66.) Bradford, 15.3.1844. (Nicoll: *Paul the Pilot; or, The Wreck of the Raven in 1692*; T. Greenwood, 9.9.1839.)

Garibaldi, the Liberator of Italy.
(*Era*, 20.1.61.) Blackburn, 16.1.1861. (Nicoll: T. Taylor, 17.10.1859, D.)

Gentleman in Black, The.
"Laughable Farce". (Playbill.) Hull, 9.10.1843. (Nicoll: M. Lemon, 9.12.1840, F.)

Gilderoy; or, The Highland Outlaw.
"Scottish Romantic Drama". (Playbill.) Hull, 23.10.1843. (Nicoll: *or, The Bonnie Boy*; W. Barrymore, Jr., 25.6.1822, MD.)

Gipsy Queen, The.
"Drama". (*Era*, 27.1.50.) Carlisle, 21.1.1850. (Nicoll lists various pieces of this title but none before 1854.)

Good-looking Fellow, The; or, The Tailor with the Roman Nose.
"Laughable Farce". (Playbill.) Drypool, 15.8.1845. (Nicoll: J. Kenney and A. Bunn, 17.4.1834.)

Grace Clairville; or, The Murder of the Symon's Yat!
"New and Successful Drama". (Playbill.) Hull, 16.10.1843. (Nicoll: A. Lewis, 20.2.1843, D.)

Green Bushes, The; or, 100 Years Ago!
"Entirely New and Original Drama". (Playbill.) Hull, 30.10.1845.
(Nicoll: J. B. Buckstone, 27.1.1845, D.)

Green Hills of the Far West, The.
"Drama". (Text, p. 111.) Halifax, 2.10.1854. (Nicoll: J. H. Wilkins, c. 1840s.)

Hamlet.
(Numerous textual references.) Earliest actual recorded performance (*Era*, 17.6.49.) Preston, June 1849. (Numerous versions of Shakespeare's text listed in Nicoll.)

Hofer, the Tell of the Tyrol.
"Grand Historical Play". (Playbill.) Hull, 25.10.1842. (Nicoll: E. Fitzball, 1.5.1830, MD.)

Holly Bush Hall.
"Drama". (*Era*, 29.4.60.) Blackburn, 25.4.1860. (Nicoll lists three versions, all 1860, D.)

Home Sweet Home; or, The Labourer and his Dog.
"Dog piece". (Text, p. 77.) Date of first perf. not known, but in repertoire by 1847. Written for Wild's by Somerset around 1846. (Not listed in Nicoll—the piece of this title under the authorship of Somerset, dated 19.3.1829 is *not* the same drama.)

House that Jack Built, The.
"Pantomime". (Text, p. 151.) Dewsbury, 30.3.1857. (Various versions listed in Nicoll, from 1821 onwards, P.)

How We Live in the World of London.
"Sensation drama". (Text, p. 140.) Halifax, Oct. or Nov. 1856. (Nicoll: J. B. Johnstone, 24.3.1856, D.)

Hunter of the Alps, The.
"Melo-Drama". (*Era*, 6.3.53.) Ashton-under-Lyne, Feb. 1853. (Nicoll: W. Dimond, 3.7.1804, MD.)

Hunting a Turtle.
"Laughable Farce". (Playbill.) Drypool, 19.8.1844. (Nicoll: C. Selby, 14.9.1835, F.)

Ice Witch, The; or, The Sea King's Bride.
"Fairy tale". (Playbill.) Wakefield, 28.6.1842. (Nicoll: ... *or, The Frozen Hand*; J. B. Buckstone, 25.3.1831, RD.)

Idiot Witness, The; or, A Tale of Blood.
(Text, p. 35.) Date of first perf. not known, but in repertoire c. 1835. (Nicoll: J. T. Haines, 6.10.1823, MD.)

Incendiaries, The; or, The Haunted Manor.
(*Era*, 20.10.61.) Wakefield, 14.10.1861. (Nicoll: unknown author, 29.8.1859, D.)

Industry and Idleness; or, The Orphan's Legacy.
"Adelphi Drama". (*Burnley Advertiser*, 5.2.59.) Burnley, 7.2.1859. (Nicoll: E. Stirling, 9.4.1846, D.)

Ingomar; or, The Sons of the Wilderness.
(*Era*, 30.1.59.) Burnley, 28.1.1859. (Nicoll: Mrs. G. W. Lovell, 9.6.1851.)

Intrigue.
"Farce". (*Era*, 25.12.53.) Bury, 19.12.1853. (Nicoll: J. Poole, 26.4.1841, Int.)

Irishman's Home, The.
"Popular Drama". (*Wigan Observer*, 19.12.57.) Wigan, Dec. 1857. (Nicoll: unknown author, May 1833, D.)

Irishman in London, The.
"Farce". (Playbill) Drypool, 8.9.1846. (Nicoll: W. Macready, 21.4.1792, F.)

Irish Tutor, The.
"Farce". (*Era*, 3.3.50.) Carlisle, 26.2.1850. (Nicoll: R. Butler, 28.10.1822, F.)

Iron Chest, The.
(Text, p. 119.) Bury, Feb. 1855. (Nicoll: G. Colman the Younger, 12.3.1796, MD.)

Isabelle; or, The Girl! The Wife! and The Mother!
"The Celebrated Domestic Drama". (Playbill.) Hull, 21.10.1844. (Nicoll: ... *or, A Woman's Life*; J. B. Buckstone, 27.1.1834, D.)

It is Never Too Late to Mend.
"Popular Prize Drama". (*Era*, 31.10.58.) Halifax, 24.10.1858. (Nicoll: no version listed before 1860.) The playbill states that this dramatisation was by J. B. Johnstone.

Jack Robinson and his Monkey.
"Nautical Piece". (*Era*, 9.5.52.) Colne, 3.5.1852. (Nicoll: W. Barrymore, 18.12.1828 or C. P. Thompson, 14.7.1828.)

Jack Sheppard.
"A New and Singularly Graphic Play". (Playbill.) Hull, 14.10.1841. (Nicoll lists several versions, those by Buckstone, Raines and Moncrieff all dating from 1839.)

Jack the Giant Killer; or, Harlequin King Arthur and Ye Knights of Ye Round Table.
"Pantomime". (*Era*, 16.9.49.) Penrith, 3.9.1849. (Nicoll lists numerous versions of *Jack* from 1803 onwards, but none with this particular alternative title.)

Jane Brightwell; or, The Beggar's Petition.
"Highly popular and domestic drama". (*Burnley Advertiser*, 18.3.1858.) Burnley, 20.12.1858. See *The Beggar's Petition.*

Jane Shore.
(Text, p. 35.) Date of first perf. not known, but in repertoire c. 1835. (Nicoll lists various versions, among them N. Rowe, 1714, and J. P. Kemble, 1815.)

Janet Pride.
(Text, p. 140.) Halifax, c. Oct. 1856. (Nicoll: D. Boucicault; first performance in England, 5.2.1855, D.)

Jemmy Green; or, What's O'Clock?
"Comic Extravaganza". (*Burnley Advertiser*, 27.11.58.) Burnley, 27.11.1858. (Not listed in Nicoll.)

Jenny Foster the Sailor's Child; or, The Winter Robin.
"Nautical Domestic Drama". (*Burnley Advertiser*, 4.12.58.) Burnley, 6.12.1858. (Nicoll: C. H. Hazlewood, Oct. 1855, D.)

Jessy Vere.
(*Era*, 11.8.61.) Wakefield, 2.8.1861. (Nicoll: C. H. Hazlewood, Feb. 1856, D.)

Jewess, The; or, The Council of Constance.
Advertised at different times as "Grand Melo-Drama" and "Historical Drama". (Text, p. 63.) Bradford, Jan. 1844. (Nicoll lists several versions, among them W. T. Moncrieff and J. R. R. Planché, both 1835, D. Spec.)

John Bull in France.
"Laughable Farce". (Playbill.) Hull, 20.10.1843. (Nicoll: unknown author, 21.8.1811, Ba.)

John Doe; or, The Peep O'Day Boys.
"Sensation piece". (*Era*, 15.3.63.) Huddersfield, 11.3.1863. (Not listed in Nicoll.) Possibly *Peep O'Day* or *Break O'Morn* (q.v.)

John Hobbs and Tim Dobbs.
"Laughable Farce". (Playbill.) Hull, 4.11.1845. (Nothing listed in Nicoll of a similar title before 1849.)

King Lear.
(Text, p. 119.) Bury, 26.2.1855. (Nicoll lists numerous versions of Shakespeare's text.)

King's Gardener, The.
"Farce". (*Era*, 19.8.48.) Kendal, 17.8.1849. (Nicoll: C. Selby, 1.4.1839, Ba.)

Kiss in the Dark, A.
"Screaming Farce". (Playbill.) Holbeck, 20.9.1859. (Nicoll: J. B. Buckstone, 13.6.1840, F.)

Lady Audley's Secret.
(Text, p. 209.) Keighley, c. Nov. 1863. (Nicoll lists three versions, all 1863: W. E. Suter 21.2; G. Roberts, 28.2; C. H. Hazlewood, 25.5, D.)

Lady of Lyons, The; or, Love and Pride.
"Sir E. L. Bulwer's beautiful play." (Playbill.) Wakefield, 24.6.1842. (Nicoll: Sir E. Bulwer-Lytton, 15.2.1838, D.)

Laid Up in Port; or, Sharks Alongside.
(Text, p. 111.) Bury, c. Dec. 1853. (Nicoll: T. H. Higgie, 10.4.1846, D.)

Lamplighter, The.
(*Era*, 9.12.55.) Wakefield, Dec. 1855. (Nicoll lists S. Davis, Newcastle, 9.1.54 and unknown author, 30.6.54, but this may have been a dramatisation by a member of the company.)

Law of Java, The; or The Death Dealer of Batavia!
"Beautiful Romantic Drama". (Playbill.) Hull, 20.10.1843. (Nicoll: G. Colman the Younger, 11.5.1822, but a comparison of playbills makes it clear that this is the same piece as *Bound 'Prentice to a Waterman*—see above.

Lear of Private Life, The; or, The Broken-Hearted Father.
"Beautiful Domestic Drama". (Playbill.) Hull, 20.10.1842. (Nicoll: W. T. Moncrieff, 27.4.1820, D.) See also *Smiles and Tears.*

Lesson for Lovers, A.
"Farce". (Playbill.) Hull, 27.10.1843. (Nicoll: *The Young Widow; or, A Lesson for Lovers*; J. T. G. Rodwell, 1.11.1824, F.) The cast list on the playbill for this piece is the same as that for *A Soldier and a Sailor*—see below.

Life and Struggles of a Working Man, The.
"Sensational drama". (Text, p. 119.) Bury, 28.3.1855. Written by C. R. Somerset. (Nicoll: unknown author, 7.11.1853, D.)

Life of a Soldier, The.
(Text, p. 168.) Burnley, Jan. 1859. (Nicoll: G. D. Pitt, Oct. 1848.)

Lion of Naples, The.
(Text, p. 162.) Wigan, 15.3.1858. (Not listed in Nicoll.) Possibly a version of *Masaniello*—see below.

Lion of the Desert, The.
"Dog piece". (Text, pp. 77–8.) Written for Wild's by Somerset c. 1846. Date of first perf. not known. (Nicoll: unknown author, 22.6.1840, Spec.)

Loss of the Royal George, The; or, The Fatal Land Breeze.
"Nautical Drama". (Playbill.) Wakefield, 29.6.1842. (Nicoll: C. Z. Barnett, 8.6.1835, MD.)

Louis XI.
(Text, p. 119.) Bury, 2.3.1855. (Nicoll: D. Boucicault, 13.1.55, D.)

Lovers' Quarrels; or, Like Master, Like Man.
"Laughable Farce". (Playbill.) Hull, 24.10.1842. (Nicoll: T. King, 1816.)

Luke the Labourer; or, The Lost Son.
(*Era*, 12.1.51.) Huddersfield, Jan. 1851. (Nicoll: J. B. Buckstone, 17.10.1826, MD.)

Macbeth; or, The Weird Sisters.
(*Oxberry's Budget*, 5.2.44.) Bradford, 27.1.1844. (Nicoll lists various versions of Shakespeare's text; this is probably Charles Dibdin the Younger's, from 1819.)

Make Your Wills.
"Screaming farce". (Text, p. 224.) Brighouse, Feb. 1865. (Nicoll: E. Mayhew & G. Smith, 16.7.1836, F.)

Manrico.
(Text, p. 224.) Dewsbury, Jan. 1865. "Founded on *Il Trovatore*." (Not listed in Nicoll.)

Margaret Catchpole, the Heroine of Suffolk!; or, The Female Horse Stealer.
(Text, p. 69.) Leeds, July 1845. (Nicoll: E. Stirling, 24.3.1845.)

Margaret's Ghost; or, The Libertine's Ship.
"Drama". (Playbill.) Hull, Oct. 1846. (Nicoll: E. Fitzball, 14.10.1833, MD.)

Marianne, the Child of Charity.
"Entirely New Drama". (Playbill.) Hull, 27.10.1845. (Nicoll: G. Dibdin Pitt, 30.12.1844, DD.)

Mariner's Dream, The; or, The Jew of Plymouth.
"New Nautical Drama". (Playbill.) Hull, 2.11.1844. (Nicoll: C. Z. Barnett, 17.10.1838, D.)

Married Bachelor, The.
"Laughable Comedietta". (Playbill.) Holbeck, 28.9.1859. (Nicoll: D. Jerrold, 4.4.1831, D.)

Married Rake, The; or, A Lesson for Husbands.
"Laughable Farce". (*Wakefield Journal*, 3.7.40.) Wakefield, 3.7.1840. (Nicoll: C. Selby, 9.2.1835, C.)

Martha Willis; or, The Perils of an Orphan Girl.
"Domestic Drama". (Playbill.) Holbeck, 29.9.1859. (Nicoll: D. Jerrold, 4.4.1831, D.)

Masaniello; or, The Fisherman of Naples.
Advertised at different times as "Beautiful Patriotic Drama" and "Musical Play". (Playbill.) Hull, 17.10.1843. (Nicoll: . . . *or, The Dumb Girl of Portici*; various versions listed, from 1829 onwards, all adapted from Scribe, MD.)

Masked Mother, The.
(*Era*, 21.7.61.) Wakefield, July 1861. (Nicoll: C. H. Hazlewood, 4.7.59, or C. Calvert, 5.12.59, D.)

Masks and Faces.
(Text, p. 129.) Blackburn, March 1856. (Nicoll: T. Taylor and C. Reade, 20.11.1852, C.)

Master Humphrey's Clock; or, Deeds and Doings in the Lone House.
"An interesting Drama from Boz's work". (Playbill.) Hull, 13.10.1842. (Nicoll: F. F. Cooper, 29.5.1840, D.)

Match in the Dark, A.
"Laughable Farce". (Playbill.) Hull, 23.10.1843. (Nicoll: C. Dance, 21.2.1833, F.)

Mazeppa.
"Horse piece". (*Era*, 20.5.49.) Blackburn, 14.5.1849. (Numerous versions listed by Nicoll, from H. M. Milner, 1823, onwards, RD.)

Meg Murnoch; or, The Mountain Hag.
"Melo-Drama". (Playbill.) Hull, Oct. 1846. (Nicoll: W. Barrymore, 20.5.1816, MD. Spec.)

Merchant of Venice, The.
(Text, p. 66.) Bradford, 21.3.1844. (Numerous versions of Shakespeare's text listed in Nicoll.)

Merry Wives of Windsor, The.
(Text, p. 119.) Bury, Feb. 1855. (Numerous versions of Shakespeare's text listed in Nicoll.)

Michael Erle the Maniac Lover; or, The Fayre Lass of Lichfield.
"Romantic Drama". (Playbill.) Drypool, 14.8.1845. (Nicoll: T. W. Wilks, 26.12.1839. RD.)

Midnight; or, The Thirteenth Chime.
"Drama". (*Era*, 13.1.50.) Carlisle, 9.1.1850. (Nicoll has *Midnight; or, The Discovery*, unknown author, 6.2.1832, D.)

Miller and his Men, The.
(Text, p. 111.) Bury, c. Dec. 1853. (Nicoll: I. Pocock, 21.10.1813, MD.)

Minnigrey.
(*Era*, 23.10.53.) Dewsbury, 18.10.1853. ". . . said to have been written expressly for this establishment." (Nicoll: J. B. Johnstone, 12.4.1852, D.)

Mr. and Mrs. Pringle.
"Laughable Farce". (Playbill.) Hull, 16.10.1843. (Nicoll: J. T. deTrueba, 9.10.1832, C.Ent.)

Mistletoe Bough, The.
"Drama". (Playbill.) Halifax, June 1837. (Nicoll: C. R. Somerset, 1834.)

Mrs. White.
"Laughable Farce". (Playbill.) Hull, 1.11.1844. (Nicoll: R. J. Raymond, 23.6.1835, Oa.)

Moors in Spain, The; or, The Horrors of the Inquisition.
(*Burnley Advertiser*, 15.1.59.) Burnley, 15.1.1859. (Nicoll: *Florinda; or, The Moors in Spain*, unknown author, 3.7.1851, O; actually MD.)

Mountain Pirate, The.
(*Era*, 11.8.61.) Wakefield, 2.8.1861. (Not listed in Nicoll.) Possibly a version of *The Bandit Merchant*—see above.

Mummy, The.
"Laughable Farce". (Playbill.) Hull, 8.10.1842. (Nicoll: W. B. Bernard, 20.5.1833, OF.)

Mungo Park; or, African Treachery (or, The Sailor and his Dogs).
"Drama". (Text, p. 76.) Lancaster, c. 1847. (Nicoll: B. Bernard, 29.6.1840, Spec.) There was also a version by C. Dibdin the Younger, 1819, under the title *Mungo Park; or, The Treacherous Guide.* Sam Wild's

addition to the title of *The Sailor and his Dogs* probably indicates some inclusion of scenes from *The Red Indian* pieces—see below.

Murderers, The.
(Playbill.) Bury, 3.2.1855. (Not listed in Nicoll.) Possibly *Peter Bell*—see below.

Mutiny at the Nore.
(Text, p. 35.) Date of first perf. not known, but in repertoire c. 1835. (Nicoll: D. W. Jerrold, 7.6.1830, MD.)

My Poll and my Partner Joe.
"Nautical drama". (Text, p. 35.) In repertoire c. 1835. (Nicoll: J. T. Haines, 31.8.1835, MD.)

My Poor Dog Tray; or, The Idiot of the Shannon.
(Text, p. 79.) Blackburn, 14.4.1849. (Nicoll lists a burletta of this title under the authorship of T. G. Blake, 7.4.1845, but the piece played at Wild's seems to have been a serious drama.)

My Precious Betsy.
"Farce". (*Era*, 13.10.1861.) Wakefield, Oct. 1861. (Nicoll: J. M. Morton, 18.2.1850, F.)

Mysteries of Paris, The.
(*Era*, 12.1.51. Huddersfield, Jan. 1851. (Nicoll: C. Dillon, 2.9.1844, MD.)

New Footman, The.
"Laughable Farce". (Playbill.) Hull, 29.10.1844. (Nicoll: C. Selby, 28.3.1842, Ba.)

New Market Butcher.
"Laughable Farce". (Playbill.) Hull, 14.10.1841. (Not listed in Nicoll.)

"No".
"Farce". (*Oxberry's Budget*, 5.2.44.) Bradford, 27.1.1844. (Nicoll: W. H. Murray, 14.11.1826 or F. Reynolds, 16.5.1828, F.)

Ocean Monarch, The; or, The Ship on Fire.
"Nautical Drama". (*Theatrical Times*, 11.11.48.) Heywood, Oct. 1848. (Nicoll: C. Somerset, 27.9.1848.)

Ocean of Life, The; or, Every Inch a Sailor.
"Highly affecting Nautical Melo-Drama". (Playbill.) Hull, 20.10.1841.
See *Every Inch a Sailor*, above.

Old Adam; or, A Father's Dream.
"Drama". (*Era*, 28.11.58.) Burnley, Nov. 1858. (Nicoll: W. T.
Townsend, 6.8.1853, D.)

Old Commodore, The.
"Farce". (*Era*, 13.1.50.) Carlisle, 7.1.1850. (Nicoll: nothing of this title
listed before 1864. *The Old Commodore, or, The Birthday* was played by
Davidge in Bristol in 1839.)

Oldham Recruit, The.
"Farce". (*Oxberry's Budget*, 26.2.44.) Bradford, 16.2.1844. (Not listed in
Nicoll.)

Old Oak Chest, The; or, The Smuggler's Son and the Robber's Daughter.
"Interesting Romantic Drama". (Playbill.) Hull, 15.10.1841. (Nicoll: J.
M. Scott, 5.2.1816, MD.)

Ostler and the Robber, The; or, The Dogs of the Chateau.
"Romantic Drama". (Text, p. 66.) Bradford, March 1844. (Nicoll: *The
Innkeeper of Abbeville; or, The Ostler and the Robber*; E. Fitzball, 6.3.1822,
MD.)

Othello.
(Text, p. 35.) In repertoire c. 1835. (Numerous versions of Shakespeare's
text listed in Nicoll.)

Our House at Home.
(Playbill.) Drypool, August 1846. (Nicoll: *Our Old House at Home*; T. G.
Blake, 26.7.1841, MD.)

Our Mary Ann.
"Laughable Farce". (Playbill.) Hull, 31.10.1843. (Nicoll: J. B. Buckstone, 18.1.1838, F.)

Out of Luck; or, His Grace the Duke.
"Laughable Farce". (Playbill.) Hull, 21.10.1842. (Nicoll: E. Stirling,
1.4.1839, Ba.)

Patriot of Rome, The.
(Text, p. 162.) Wigan, 15.3.1858. (Not listed in Nicoll.) Possibly a version of *Brutus* or *Virginius*—see above and below.

Peep o'Day; or Savourneen Deelish.
"Sensation drama". (Text, p. 222.) Dewsbury, 10.10.1864. (Nicoll: E. Falconer, 9.11.1861, D.)

Peter Bell the Waggoner; or, The Murderers of Massaic.
"Domestic Drama". (Playbill.) Hull, 24.10.1844. (Nicoll: J. B. Buckstone, 20.4.1829, MD.)

Pilot, The.
(*Oxberry's Budget*, 8.1.44.) Bradford, 31.12.1843. (Various adaptations of Cooper's novel listed in Nicoll, from E. Fitzball, 1825, onwards.)

Pilot's Grave, The.
(*Era*, 4.8.61.) Wakefield, 29.7.1861. (Not listed in Nicoll.) Campbell's travelling theatre performed *The Pilot's Grave; or, A Storm at Sea* at Hartlepool in 1843. Possibly a version of *The Pilot.*

Pirate Ship, The; or, The Dog(s) of the Wave.
"Nautical Drama". (*Era*, 30.12.49.) Carlisle, 24.12.1849. "Written expressly for Nelson"; possibly by Somerset. (Not listed in Nicoll.)

Pizarro; or, The Death of Rolla.
(*Era*, 3.3.50.) Carlisle, 25.2.1850. (Various versions listed in Nicoll; probably R. B. Sheridan, 24.5.1799, T.)

P.P.; or, The Man and the Tiger.
(Playbill.) Drypool, 21.8.1843. (Nicoll: T. Parry, 21.10.1833, F.)

Prophet of the Moor, The; or, The Druid's Stone.
"Romantic Drama". (Playbill.) Wakefield, 28.6.1842. (Nicoll: . . . or, the *Fire Raiser*; G. Almar, 21.2.1831, MD.)

Quarter-Day; or, How to Pay Rent Without Money.
"Laughable Farce". (Playbill.) Hull, 21.10.1844. (Nicoll: unknown author, 15.4.1811, Ba.)

Queer Subject, The.
"Laughable Farce". (Playbill.) Hull, 17.10.1843. (Nicoll: J. S. Coyne, 28.11.1836, F.)

Raby Rattler; or, The Progress of a Scamp.
"Drama". (*Theatrical Times*, 11.11.48.) Heywood, Oct. 1848. (Various versions listed in Nicoll; probably E. Stirling, 3.2.1847, D.)

Railroad Station, The.
"Laughable Farce". (Playbill.) Wakefield, 24.6.1842. (Nicoll: T. E. Wilks, 3.10.1840, Ba.)

Raising the Wind.
"Laughable Farce". (Text, p. 24.) Leeds, c. 1830. (Nicoll: J. Kenney, 5.11.1803.)

Rajah's Daughter, The; or, The Battle of Amedabad.
"Grand Eastern Spectacle". (*Burnley Advertiser*, 11.12.58.) Burnley, 13.12.1858. See *The War in India.*

Raymond and Agnes; or, The Castle of Lindenbergh.
(*Era*, 17.6.49.) Preston, June 1849. (Nicoll: M. G. Lewis, 22.11.1809, MD.)

Red Barn, The; or, The Murder of Maria Marten.
"Interesting Drama". (Playbill.) Halifax, 28.6.1837. (Nicoll: T. Mildenhall, 23.11.1829; or, unknown author, 27.10.1830.)

Red Indian, The; or, The Sailor and his Dog(s).

Red Indian, The; or, The Dog(s) of the Wreck.

Red Indian and his Dog(s), The.
Probably all versions of the same piece. (Text, p. 66, 74, etc.) In repertoire before 1846. (Nicoll lists two versions by unknown authors, both based on Selkirk's story: *The Red Indian; or, Selkirk and his Dog*, 26.8.1822 and *The Red Indian; or, The Shipwrecked Mariner and his Faithful Dogs*, 9.3.1824. He also lists a piece under the title of *The Cherokee Chief; or, The Dogs of the Wreck*, unknown author, 1833.)

Red Lance, The; or, The Merrie Men of Hoxton.
(Text, p. 62.) In repertoire c. 1844. (Nicoll: E. R. Lancaster, 1841.)

Review, The; or, The Wags of Windsor.
"Laughable Farce". (Playbill.) Drypool, 18.8.1845. (Nicoll: G. Colman the Younger, 2.9.1800, O.F.)

Richard III.
(Text, p. 21, 115, etc.) First recorded perf. Bury, Jan. 1855, but probably in repertoire considerably earlier. (Numerous versions of Shakespeare's text listed in Nicoll.)

Richelieu.
(Text, p. 119.) Bury, 17.2.1854. (Nicoll: E. Bulwer-Lytton, 7.3.1839, D.)

Robert the Bruce.
(Text, p. 111.) Bury, c. Nov. 1853. (Nicoll: unknown author, 24.5.1819, MD.)

Rob Roy; or, Scotland in Olden Times.
"Pocock's Celebrated Play". (Text, p. 21, etc.) In repertoire c. 1832. (Nicoll: I. Pocock, 3/1818.)

Romeo and Juliet.
(*Era*, 2.3.51.) Huddersfield, Feb. 1851. (Numerous versions of Shakespeare's text listed in Nicoll.)

Rose of Ettrick Vale, The.
(Text, p. 62.) In repertoire c. 1844. (Nicoll: T. J. Lynch, 23.5.1825.)

Rover's Bride, The; or, The Pirate of the Spanish Main.
"Nautical Drama". (Playbill.) Hull, 26.10.1842. (Nicoll: ... or, The Bittern's Swamp; G. Almar, 30.10.1830, MD.)

Ruth; or, The Lass that Loved a Sailor.
"Nautical Drama". (Playbill.) Hull, 9.10.1843. (Nicoll: J. T. Haines, 23.1.1843.)

Ruthven the Smuggler.
(*Era*, 7.4.50.) Carlisle, April 1850. (Not listed in Nicoll.) Possibly a version of *The Mariner's Dream*—see above.

Sadak and Kalesrade.
"Grand spectacle". (Text, p. 202.) Huddersfield, c. May 1863. (Nicoll lists T. J. Dibdin, c. 1794, unknown author 1814 and M. R. Mitford, 20.4.1835, but Stirling in his memoirs says he also wrote a version.)

St. Clair of the Isles; or, The Outlaws of Barra.
"Grand Scottish Drama". (Playbill.) Holbeck, 28.9.1859. (Nicoll: E. Polack, 16.4.1838.)

Sarah's Young Man.
"Screaming farce". (*Burnley Advertiser*, 13.11.58.) Burnley, 13.11.1858.
(Nicoll: W. E. Suter, 21.4.1856, F.)

Scandal Hath a Busy Tongue.
"Very lively farce". (Text, p. 27.) Leeds, 25.11.1835. (Not listed in Nicoll.)

Sea, The; or, The Ocean Child.
(Text, p. 35.) In repertoire by 1835. (Nicoll: C. A. Somerset, 18.5.1842, but copy in Bodleian library gives year of first performance as 1834. ND.)

Sea Captain, The, and the Lady of Lambythe; or, A Bridal Three Centuries Ago.
"Beautiful Drama". (Playbill.) Hull, 31.10.1843. (Nicoll: *The Lady of Lambethe; or, A Bridal Three Centuries Back*; T. E. Wilks, 5.8.1839, D.) E. Bulwer-Lytton also wrote a drama called *The Sea-Captain*, 31.10.39, but a comparison of his text with the playbill makes this unlikely to have been the same piece.

Sea-King's Vow, The; or, The Struggle for Liberty.
(*Era*, 2.9.49.) Kendal, 29.8.1849. (Nicoll: E. Stirling, 16.2.1846, D.)

Sea of Ice, The; or, The Wild Flower of Mexico and the Struggle for Gold.
(Text, p. 120.) Blackburn, 23.4.1855. (Nicoll: *The Thirst of Gold; or, The Lost Ship and the Wild Flower of Mexico*; B. Webster, 5.12.1853.)

Sepoy Revolt, The.
(*Era*, 28.2.58.) Wigan, Feb. 1858. See *The Storming of Delhi.*

Shade, The; or, Blood for Blood.
(*Burnley Advertiser*, 12.2.59.) Burnley, 12.2.1859. (Nicoll: C. P. Thompson, 22.8.29, MD.)

Sharp and Flat.
"Farce". (*Oxberry's Budget*, 8.1.44.) Bradford, Jan. 1844. See *Flat & Sharp.*

Showman and his Monkey, The.
"Comic Extravaganza". (Playbill.) Holbeck, 6.10.1859. (Not listed in Nicoll.)

Siamese Twins, The.
"Laughable Farce". (Text, p. 63.) Bradford, Jan. 1844. (Nicoll: G. A. A'Beckett, 14.4.1834, F.)

Siege of Berwick, The; or, The Red Hall.
"Historical Drama". (*Era*, 23.2.62.) Huddersfield, 17.2.1862. (Nicoll: E. Jerningham, 13.11.1793 or J. Miller, 1824, T.)

Siege of Cawnpore, The.
(Preston Guardian, 29.5.58.) Preston, May 1858. See *The Storming of Delhi.*

Sir Roderic of the Rhine; or, The Nymphs in Revolt.
"Pantomime". (*Era*, 11.1.57.) Dewsbury, Dec. 1856 or Jan. 1857. (Not listed in Nicoll.) See also *The Water Nymphs' Revolt.*

Sixteen-String Jack; or, The Last of the Highwaymen.
"Drama". (Playbill.) Drypool, 9.9.1846. (Nicoll: W. L. Rede, 18.2.1823, Spec. or T. E. Wilks, 28.11.1842, MD.)

Slasher and Crasher.
"Farce". (*Huddersfield Chronicle*, 4.1.51.) Huddersfield, 6.1.1851. (Nicoll: J. M. Morton, 13.11.1848, F.)

Slave, The; or, The Blessings of Liberty.
"Dog piece". (Text, p. 77.) Written for Wild's by C. R. Somerset. In repertoire c. 1846. (Nicoll lists a piece of this title under the authorship of T. Morton, 12.11.1816.)

Slave's Revenge, The; or, The Planter and his Dogs.
(*Era*, 24.11.61.) Wakefield, 20.11.1861. (Nicoll: *The Foulahs; or, A Slave's Revenge*; W. Barrymore, 26.8.1823, MD.) A poster for Mr. Cony and his dogs Hector and Bruin at Halifax, dated 1839, claims that this piece was written expressly for them.

Smiles and Tears; or, The Broken-Hearted Father.
"Pathetic Drama". (Playbill.) Holbeck, 4.10.1859. See *The Lear of Private Life.*

Smoked Miser, The.
"Laughable Farce". (Playbill.) Hull, 19.10.1847. (Nicoll: D. Jerrold, June 1823, Int.)

Smuggler's Son and the Robber's Daughter, The.
(*Era*, 13.1.50.) Carlisle, 7.1.1850. See *The Old Oak Chest.*

Snowstorm, The.
(Playbill.) Bury, 2.2.1855. (Not listed in Nicoll; possibly *The Fatal Snowstorm*, W. Barrymore, c. 1820 or unknown author 20.3.1854.)

Soldier and a Sailor, A; or, A Lesson in Love.
"Laughable Farce". (Playbill.) Hull, 1.11.1843. (Nicoll: A. McLaren, 1805, M.Ent.) See also *A Lesson for Lovers.*

Spirit Rapping and Table Moving.
"Somerset's new farce". (*Era*, 22.1.54.) Bury, Jan. 1854. (Nicoll: unknown author, 4.7.1853.)

Spitfire, The; or, Men of Wars Men.
"Laughable Nautical Drama". (Playbill.) Hull, 26.10.1842. (Nicoll: J. M. Morton, 13.9.1837, Ext.)

State Secrets; or, The Tailor of Tamworth.
"Laughable Farce". (Playbill.) Hull, 10.10.1843. (Nicoll: T. E. Wilks, 12.9.1836, Ba.)

Statue Gallery, The; or, A Model Venus.
"Laughable farce". (Playbill.) Bury, 2.2.1855. (Not listed in Nicoll.)

Storming of Delhi, The.
(Text, pp. 161–2.) Wigan, 15.2.1858. Written for Wild's by Somerset. (Nicoll lists *The Siege and Capture of Delhi*, unknown author, at Astley's 23.11.1857, Equest. Spec.) Also played under the title of *The Fall of Delhi, The Siege of Cawnpore* and *The Sepoy Revolt.*

Stranger, The.
(Text, p. 21, etc.) In repertoire c. 1832. (Nicoll: B. Thompson, 24.3.1798 plus several unknown authors, all adapted from Kotzebue, D.)

Susan Hopley; or, The Trials and Vicissitudes of a Servant Girl, And the Murder at the Old Manor House.
"Admired Domestic Drama". (Playbill.) Drypool, 18.8.1845. (Nicoll: G. Dibdin Pitt, 31.5.1841, DD.)

Tables Turned, The; or, Master Humphrey and his Clock.
(Text, p. 62.) Probably in repertoire c. 1844. (Nicoll: E. R. Lancaster, date unknown, F.) Printed in *Oxberry's Budget* 11.7.1843.

Taming of the Shrew, The.
(Text, p. 119.) Bury, 26.3.1855. (Various versions of Shakespeare's text listed in Nicoll.)

Temptation; or, The Devil's Daughter.
(*Era*, 9.12.55.) Wakefield, Dec. 1855. (Nicoll: G. A. A'Beckett, 1837; J. P. Wilson, 1841; W. T. Townsend, 1842.)

Thackeen Dhu.
"Irish Drama". (Text, p. 202.) Huddersfield, 16.3.1863. (Not listed in Nicoll.)

Ticket-of-Leave Man, The.
(Text, p. 223.) Dewsbury, 16.12.1864. (Nicoll: T. Taylor, 27.5.1863, D.)

Tiger at Large, The; or, The Cad of the Buss.
"Farce". (Playbill.) Hull, 28.10.1845. (Nicoll: unknown author, 8.5.1837, Ba.)

Timor [sic] the Tartar.
"Horse piece". (Text, p. 187.) Blackburn, c. March 1860. (Nicoll: M. G. lewis, 29.4.1811, MD.)

Tom Cringle's Log; or, Mat of the Iron Hand.
"Nautical Drama". (Playbill.) Hull, 19.10.1842. (Nicoll: E. Fitzball, 26.5.1834, D.)

Tom the Piper's Son.
"Comic Pantomime". (Playbill.) Hull, 13.10.1842. (Nothing of this title listed in Nicoll before 1875.)

True and False Heiress, The.
(*Era*, 9.12.55.) Wakefield, Dec. 1855. (Not listed in Nicoll.)

Turning the Tables.
"Laughable Farce". (*Oxberry's Budget*, 26.2.44.) Bradford, 17.2.1844. (Nicoll: J. Poole, 11.11.1830, F.)

'Twas I!
(Text, p. 226.) Halifax, c. July 1865. (Nicoll: J. H. Payne, 3.12.1825, OF.)

Two Bonnycastles, The.
"Laughable Farce". (*Burnley Advertiser*, 13.11.58.) Burnley, 16.11.1858. (Nicoll: J. M. Morton, 25.11.1851, F.)

Two Eyes for Two.
"Comic Extravaganza". (*Burnley Advertiser*, 15.1.59.) Burnley, 17.1.1859. (Nicoll: *Two Eyes Between Two; or, Pay Me for my Eye*; D. W. Jerrold, 13.10.1828, Ext.)

Two Gregories, The.
"Farce". (*Oxberry's Budget*, 8.1.44.) Bradford, Jan. 1844. (Nicoll: T. J. Dibdin, 23.4.1821, OF.)

Two Loves and a Life.
"Haymarket Drama". (*Era*, 1.2.57.) Dewsbury, Jan. 1857. (Nicoll: T. Taylor and C. Reade, 20.3.1854, D.)

Uncle Tom's Cabin.
(*Era*, 7.11.52.) Halifax, end Oct. 1852. "Written by a member of the company." (Numerous versions listed in Nicoll, earliest London perf. 13.9.1852.)

Unfinished Gentleman, The.
"Laughable and Fashionable Farce". (Playbill.) Hull, 18.10.1842. (Nicoll: C. Selby, 1.12.1834, Ba.)

Vagrant, his Wife and Family, The.
(*Oxberry's Budget*, 26.2.44.) Bradford, 14.2.1844. (Nicoll lists a version by an unknown author, 30.6.1845, but this is too late.)

Valentine and Orson; or, The Wild Man of the Woods.
"Interesting Romantic Drama". (Playbill.) Hull, 27.10.1842. (Nicoll: T. Dibdin, 3.4.1804, MD.)

Valsha the Slave Queen.
(*Era*, 7.4.50.) Carlisle, April 1850. (Nicoll: J. S. Coyne, 30.10.1837, incorrectly classed as Ba; it is MD.)

Village Lawyer, The.
"Farce". (Text, p. 15.) Halifax, c. 1825. (Nicoll: W. Macready, 28.8.1787, F.)

Virginius.
(*Era*, 20.2.59.) Burnley, Feb. 1859. (Nicoll: J. S. Knowles, 4/1820, T.)

Wags of Windsor, The.
(*Era*, 13.10.61.) Wakefield, Oct. 1861. See *The Review*.

Walter Tyrrel; or, The Death of William the Second.
"Grand Historical Play". (Playbill.) Hull, 27.10.1842. (Nicoll: E. Fitzball, 16.5.1837, T.)

Wanted, 1000 Milliners for the Gold Diggings!
"Farce". (Playbill.) Holbeck, 4.10.1859. (Nicoll: J. S. Coyne, 2.10.1852.)

War in India, The; or, The Rajah's Daughter.
"Dramatic Spectacle". (*Era*, 27.1.50.) Carlisle, 22.1.1850. (Nicoll: *The Cataract of the Ganges; or, The Rajah's Daughter*; W. T. Moncrieff, 27.10.1823.) Also played as *The Rajah's Daughter; or, The Battle of Amedabad.*

Wars of Napoleon, The; or, The Soldier's Bride.
"New Melodramatic Anecdote". (Playbill.) Bury, 2.2.1855. See *The Battle of Austerlitz.*

Water Queen, The; or, Harlequin and the Spirit of the Deep.
"Comic pantomine". (*Preston Guardian*, 3.6.57.) Preston, May 1857. (Nicoll: . . . *or, The Spirits of Donan, the Goblin Page*; unknown author, 8.6.1835.)

Water Nymphs' Revolt, The.
"Christmas pantomime". (Text, p. 142.) Dewsbury, Dec. 1856. See *Sir Roderic of the Rhine.*

Weathercock, The.
"Farce". (*Oxberry's Budget*, 26.2.44.) Bradford, 12.2.1844. (Nicoll: J. T. Allingham, 18.11.1805, F.)

Weaver of Lyons, The.
"Comedietta". (*Burnley Advertiser*, 11.12.58.) Burnley, 11.12.1858. (Nicoll: . . . *or, The Three Conscripts*; J. T. Barber, 24.11.1844.)

Wet Nurse, The.
"Farce". (*Era*, 20.10.61.) Wakefield, 14.10.1861. (Nicoll: unknown author, 20.4.1840, F.)

White Slave, The; or, The Flag of Freedom.
(Text, p. 111.) Bury, Dec. 1853. (Nicoll: E. Stirling, 10.8.1849, D.)

Wife, The: A Tale of Mantua.
(Text, p. 143.) Dewsbury, 1857. (Nicoll: J. S. Knowles, 24.4.1833, T.)

Wild Flower of Erin, The.
(*Era*, 15.3.63.) Huddersfield, 13.3.1863. (Not listed in Nicoll.) Possibly a version of *The Sea of Ice* (q.v.)

Wilfrid Clitheroe; or, The Husband of Two Wives!
"Domestic Drama". (Playbill.) Holbeck, 20.9.1859. (Not listed in Nicoll; cast details on playbill indicate that it is probably a version of *Kate Wynsley, Cottage Girl*, T. E. Wilks, 22.4.1845.)

Will and the Way, The.
"Drama". (Text, p. 111.) Blackburn, 1.5.1854. (Nicoll lists various versions from G. D. Pitt, 23.4.1853, onwards, D.)

William Tell.
(Text, p. 21.) In repertoire c. 1832. (Nicoll: J. S. Knowles, 11.5.1825, D.)

Wizard of the Wave, The; or, The Phantom Ship of the Avenger.
"Beautiful Nautical Drama". (Playbill.) Hull, 31.10.1842. (Nicoll: J. T. Haines, 7.9.1840, D.)

Wolf's Glen, The; or, The Seven Charmed Bullets.
"Romantic Drama". (Playbill.) Hull, 21.10.1843. (Nicoll: *Der Freischutz; or, The Demon of the Wolf's Glen and the Seven Charmed Bullets*; E. Fitzball, 6.9.1824, MD.)

Woman of the World, The.
(Text, p. 168.) Burnley, Jan. 1859. (Nicoll: C. Cavendish, 13.11.1858, D.)

Wonder, The: A Woman Keeps a Secret.
"Comedy". (*Wigan Observer*, 23.1.58.) Wigan, 28.1.1858. (Nicoll: S. Centlivre, 1714, C.)

Wood Demon, The.
(*Era*, 20.5.49.) Blackburn, May 1849. (Nicoll: *One o'Clock; or, The Knight and the Wood Demon*j; C. Kenny and A. R. Smith, 6.5.1847, Bsq. Ext.)

Young England.
"Farce". (*Era*, 13.10.61.) Wakefield, Oct. 1861. (Nicoll: J. M. Morton, 30.11.1844, F.)

Zelina; or, The Heroine of the Cross.
"Drama". (Playbill.) Hull, Oct. 1846. (Not listed in Nicoll under this title, but possibly *Zelma; or, The Triumph of the Greeks*; C. Somerset, 1830.)

APPENDIX C

GUEST STARS AT WILD'S

Date	Location	Name(s)	Other Details
11–16 Nov. 1850.	Huddersfield	"Boz's Juba"	Black singer/dancer. Research has failed to unearth any link with Dickens.
2–7 Dec. 1850	Huddersfield	Mdlle. Angelina & Mr. Mathewman	"The fascinating danseuse" and "the pantomimist".
9–14 Dec. 1850	Huddersfield	"Herr" Teasdale, W. S. Hallin	The man-monkey. Of the Queen's Theatre Hull.
		J. S. Fraser	Of the Theatre, Aberdeen.
27 Feb.– 1 Mar. 1851	Huddersfield	Herr Schmidt	"The youthful Hercules". One-armed strong man.
Dec. 1853	Bury	R. B. Hughes	Played *Hamlet*.
20–25 Feb. 1854	Bury	George Owen	Played *Hamlet, Macbeth, The Stranger, Merchant of Venice, Richelieu, The Merry Wives of Windsor*.
22–27 Jan. 1855	Bury	Butler Wentworth	Played *Hamlet, Macbeth, Richard III, Othello*.
29 Jan.– 3 Feb. 1855	Bury	Watkins Burroughs	*Rob Roy, Jock Muir, William Tell, The Wars of Napoleon, Masaniello*.
5–10 Feb. 1855	Bury	Mr. & Mrs. J. Stephens	"Formerly of Astley's".

Date	Place	Performer	Notes
26 Feb.–3 Mar. 1855	Bury	George Owen	"Six farewell nights prior to his departure for America". Played *King Lear*, *The Iron Chest*, *The Merry Wives of Windsor*, *Othello*, *Louis XI*, *Richelieu*.
5–10 Feb. 1856	Dewsbury	George Owen	
12–15 Mar. 1856	Dewsbury	George Owen	
26–31 Jan. 1857	Dewsbury	George Owen	Played *King Lear*, *Two Loves and a Life*, *Master Radcliffe*, *Henry VIII*, *Hamlet*, *The Merry Wives of Windsor*.
10–15 Feb. 1857	Dewsbury	Henry Nicholls	Tragedian and Shakespearean reader.
23–28 Feb. 1857	Dewsbury	Arthur Nelson & Miss St. Clair	Clown Vocalist who travelled with Nelson. (According to *The Era*, business had not been good in the previous weeks, hence possibly the choice of a clown.)
9–14 Mar. 1857	Dewsbury	Harvey Teasdale & his daughters	Man monkey & dancers.
16–21 Mar. 1857	Dewsbury	J. C. Cowper	"Formerly leading actor at the Amphitheatre, Liverpool." Played *Hamlet*.
c. Jan. 1858	Wigan	Henry Nicholls	
10–15 Jan. 1859	Burnley	McKean Buchanan	Played *Hamlet*, *Rob Roy*, *Macbeth*, *Othello*, *The Stranger/Richard III*, *The Moors in Spain*.

Date	Town	Performer	Notes
17–22 Jan. 1859	Burnley	T. H. Glenney	Played *The Black Doctor, Belphegor, Eustace Baudin, The Life of a Soldier, The Woman of the World.*
31 Jan.–5 Feb. 1859	Burnley	J. C. Coleman	Played *Hamlet, The Stranger, Don Cesar de Bazan, Belphegor, Catherine Howard The Corsican Brothers* and *Picarro.*
14–19 Feb. 1859	Burnley	McKean Buchanan	Return visit. Played *King Lear, Richelieu, Virginius, Brutus, The Lady of Lyons, The Merchant of Venice/Pizarro, Damon & Pythias.*
21–26 Mar. 1859	Burnley	Henry Loraine	"Pronounced by the Press to be the best Shakespearean Actor seen for the last 20 years"(*Burnley Advertiser*, 19.3.59).
c. Jan. 1860	Keighley	McKean Buchanan & Miss Fanny Rayner	3 nights at Buchanan's special request.
23–28 Apl. 1860	Blackburn	Edmondson Shirra	Tragedian. Semi-permanent theatre, moved here from Keighley.
May 1860	Blackburn	Lilia Ross	Child actress.
3–8 Dec. 1860	Blackburn	W. Patterson	Man-monkey.
4–9 Nov. 1861	Wakefield	James Holloway	
6–11 Jan. 1862	Huddersfield	Lilia Ross	

Date	Place	Performer	Notes
3–8 Feb. 1862	Huddersfield	Violet Campbell & Alfred Ramsden	Played *Hamlet, Romeo & Juliet.*
24 Feb.–1 Mar. 1862	Huddersfield	Percy Roselle	The Infant Roscius. Child actor.
24–29 Mar. 1862	Huddersfield	T. Swinbourne	*Othello.*
9–14 Feb. 1863	Huddersfield	James Holloway	Played *Break O'Morn, Richard III*, and other Shakespearian parts.
9–14 Mar. 1863	Huddersfield	W. R. Waldron	
23–28 Mar. 1863	Huddersfield	George Owen	Played *Thackeen Dhu, Richelieu, King Lear.*
30 Mar.–15 Apl. 1863	Huddersfield	Percy Roselle	Played *The Four Mowbrays* and Shakespeare.
12–17 Dec. 1864	Dewsbury	Frank Newman George Nelson	From the Royal Amphitheatre, Liverpool. From the Theatre Royal, Leeds.
19–24 Dec. 1864	Dewsbury	James Holloway	Played *Macbeth, Othello, The Hunchback of Notre Dame, Pizarro, Mazeppa, Richard III.*

BIBLIOGRAPHY

ABRAM, W. A., "Social Condition & Political Prospects of the Lancashire Workman" in *Fortnightly Review*, Oct. 1868.

ADDISON, W., *English Fairs & Markets*, 1953.

—— *The Old Roads of England*, 1980.

ANDERSON, M., *Family Structure in 19th Century Lancashire*, 1971.

ARTHUR, T., *The Life of Billy Purvis*, 1875.

ARUNDELL, D., *The Story of Sadler's Wells*, 1965.

BAINES, E., *History, Directory & Gazetteer of the County of York*, 1822.

—— *Lancashire & Cheshire Past & Present*, 1867.

BARKER, K., *Bristol at Play*, 1976.

—— "Thirty Years of Struggle" in *Theatre Notebook*, 1985. I–III.

BOOTH, M., *English Melodrama*, 1965.

BOSTOCK, E. H., *Menageries, Circuses & Theatres*, 1927.

BRADBY, D., JAMES, L., & SHARRATT, B. (eds), *Performance & Politics in Popular Drama*, 1980.

BRAITHWAITE, D., *Travelling Fairs*, 1971.

—— *Fairground Architecture*, 1968.

BRATTON, J. S., "Theatre of War" in Bradby, James & Sharratt, *Performance & Politics in Popular Drama*, 1980.

BRIGGS, A., *The Age of Improvement*, 1959.

—— *Victorian Cities*, 1963.

BUER, M. C., *Health, Wealth & Population in the Early Days of the Industrial Revolution*, 1968.

BURNETT, J. (ed.), *Useful Toil*, 1974.

CLARKE, J. (ed.), *Working Class Culture*, 1979.

COLE, G. D. H. & POSTGATE, R., *The Common People 1746–1946*, 1938.

COLEMAN, J. C., *Fifty Years of an Actor's Life*, 1904.

CORRIGAN, E., *Ups & Downs & Roundabouts*, 1972.

CORYTON, J., *Stageright*, 1873.

CROFT-COOKE, R. (ed.), *The Circus Book*, 1940.

CROSS, G., *Next Week East Lynne*, 1977.

CRUMP, J., "A Study of the Theatre Royal, Leicester" in *Theatre Notebook*, 1984.

CUNNINGHAM, H., *Leisure in the Industrial Revolution*, 1980.

DALLAS, D., *The Travelling People*, 1971.

DELGADO, A., *The Annual Outing & Other Excursions*, 1977.

DICKENS, C., *Sketches by Boz*, 1836.

DISRAELI, B., *Sybil: or, The Two Nations*, 1845.

DONAJGRODSKI, A. P. (ed.), *Social Control in 19th Century Britain*, 1977.

EGAN, P., *The Life of an Actor*, 1825.

ENGELS, F., *The Condition of the Working Classes in England*, 1892.

FARWELL, B., *Queen Victoria's Little Wars*, 1973.

FENWICK, A. J., *Travelling Shows* (MS), 1939, Fenwick Coll. Newcastle.

FIELDEN, J., *The Curse of the Factory System*, 1836.
GREEN, W., *The Life & Adventures of a Cheapjack*, 1876.
HILDESHEIMER, S., *Travelling with Wombwell's Menagerie*, n.d., c. 1912.
HILEY, M., *Victorian Working Women*, 1979.
HONE, W., *Hone's Everyday Book*, 1825.
HOPKINS, E., *A Social History of the English Working Classes 1815–1945*, 1979.
JACKSON, B., "Barnstorming Days" in *Studies in English Theatre History*, 1952.
JEROME, J. K., *On the Stage and Off*, 1885.
KING, R., *North Shields Theatres*, 1948.
LLOYD, J., *My Circus Life*, 1925.
LONGMATE, N., *King Cholera*, 1966.
—— *The Workhouse*, 1974.
—— *Milestones in Working Class History*, 1975.
—— *The Hungry Mills*, 1978.
McCUTCHEON, M. L., *Yorkshire Fairs & Markets*, 1940.
McKECHNIE, S., *Popular Entertainment Through the Ages*, 1940.
MAHARD, M. R., *The Fortunes of a Penny Showman*, Harvard 1982.
MALCOLMSON, R. W., *Popular Recreations in English Society 1700–1850*, 1973.
MANDER, R., & MITCHENSON, J., *Victorian & Edwardian Entertainment*, 1978.
MANCHESTER STATISTICAL SOCIETY, *Report on the Condition of the Working Classes*, 1834/35/36.
MARSHALL, D., *Industrial England 1766–1851*, 1972.
—— *Lancashire*, 1974.
MAYER, D., & RICHARDS, K. (eds.), *Western Popular Theatre*, 1977.
MAYHEW, H., *London Labour & the London Poor*, 1851.
MELFORD, M., *My Life in a Booth & Something More*, 1913.
MELLER, H. E., *Leisure & the Changing City 1870–1914*, 1976.
MILLER, D. P., *The Life of a Showman*, 1863.
MUNCEY, R. W., *Our Old English Fairs*, 1935.
ODELL, G. C. D., *Shakespeare from Betterton to Irving*, 1920.
OWENS, *Owens' Book of Fairs*, 1780.
PAGE, J., "Manchester Fairs", *Manchester Lit. Club Papers*, 1876.
PATERSON, P. (pseud. of Bertram, J. G.), *Glimpses of Real Life*, 1864.
PERKIN, H., *The Origins of Modern English Society 1780–1880*, 1969.
PIMLOTT, J. A. R., *The Englishman's Holiday*, 1947.
PLANCHE, J. R. R., *Recollections & Reflections*, 1901.
PORRITT, A., *It Happened Here*, 1955.
PRICE, C., *The English Theatre in Wales*, 1948.
REACH, A. B., *Manchester & the Textile Districts in 1849*, rep.1 1972.
ROSENFELD, S., *The Theatre of the London Fairs in the Eighteenth Century*, 1960.
ROWELL, G., *The Victorian Theatre*, 1956.
SABBATTINI, N., *Patrica di Fabricar Scene*, 1638, quoted in Gascoigne, B., *World Theatre*, 1968.
SANGER, G., *Seventy Years a Showman*, 1910.
SANGER COLEMAN, G., *The Sanger Story*, 1956.
SAXON, A. H., *Enter Foot & Horse*, 1978.
—— *The Life & Art of Andrew Ducrow*, 1978.
—— "The Tyranny of Charity" in *19th Century Theatre Research*, 1973.
SCOTT, C. & HOWARD, C., *The Life & Reminiscences of E. L. Blanchard*, 1898.
SCOTT, H., *The Early Doors*, 1943.
SHERIDAN, P., *Penny Theatres of Victorian London*, 1981.

SLATER, T., *Reminiscences of an Actor's Life*, 1892.
SMITH, A., *A Little Talk about Science & the Show Folks*, 1855.
SOUTHERN, R., *The Victorian Theatre*, 1970.
SPEAIGHT, G., *The History of the Circus*, 1984.
—— (ed.) *The Life & Times of Richard Barnard*, 1981.
STARSMORE, I., *English Fairs*, 1975.
STIRLING, E., *Old Drury Lane*, 1881.
SUTTON, G., *Fish and Actors*, N. Y., 1925.
TAYLOR, A. J., *The Standard of Living in Britain in the Industrial Revolution*, 1975.
THOMIS, M. I., *The Town Labourer & the Industrial Revolution*, 1974.
TRAIES, J., *Fair Booths & Fit Ups*, 1980.
TREBLE, J. H., *Urban Poverty in Britain 1830–1914*, 1979.
TREWIN, J. C., *The Pomping Folk*, 1968.
TYRWHITT-DRAKE, G., *The English Circus & Fairground*, 1946.
VANDENHOFF, G., *An Actor's Notebook*, 1865.
WAITES, B., BENNETT, T., & MARTIN, G. (eds.), *Popular Culture Past & Present*, 1982.
WARWICK, L., *Drama That Smelled*, 1975.
WHISTLER, L., *The English Festivals*, 1947.
WILKIE COLLINS, W., *Rambles Beyond Railways*, 1851.
WILLSON DISHER, M., *Fairs, Circuses & Music Halls*, 1942.

INDEX